LATINO COMMUNITIES

EMERGING VOICES
POLITICAL, SOCIAL, CULTURAL, AND LEGAL ISSUES

edited by

ANTOINETTE SEDILLO LOPEZ
UNIVERSITY OF NEW MEXICO

A GARLAND SERIES

SPANISH AND ACADEMIC ACHIEVEMENT AMONG MIDWEST MEXICAN YOUTH

THE MYTH OF THE BARRIER

———————————

PATRICIA MACGREGOR-MENDOZA

GARLAND PUBLISHING, INC.
A MEMBER OF THE TAYLOR & FRANCIS GROUP
NEW YORK & LONDON / 1999

Library of Congress Cataloging-in-Publication Data

MacGregor-Mendoza, Patricia, 1963–
    Spanish and academic achievement among Midwest Mexican
youth : the myth of the barrier / Patricia MacGregor-Mendoza.
        p.   cm. — (Latino communities)
    Includes bibliographical references and index.
    ISBN 0-8153-3345-5 (alk. paper)
    1. Mexican American youth—Education—Middle West Case
studies. 2. Language arts—Middle West Case studies. 3. Spanish
language—Study and teaching—Middle West Case studies.
4. Academic achievement—Middle West Case studies.   I. Title.
II. Series.
LC2672.4.M33 1999
371.82968'7'073—dc21
                                                    99-18527

Printed on acid-free, 250-year-life paper
Manufactured in the United States of America

Para mi marido Manuel
Te agradezco tu interminable apoyo, fe y cariño

Contents

Tables   ix
Introduction   xi

Chapter 1: Language and Academic Achievement   3
Chapter 2: Statement of the Problem   25
Chapter 3: Methodology   29
Chapter 4: Variables Related to Academic Achievement   45
Chapter 5: Mexicans, Spanish and Academic Success   79

Appendix of Research Materials   91
Bibliography   163
Index   175

Tables

Table 1.   Three most common ethnic terms identified by
           informants   48
Table 2.   Parents' occupations   49
Table 3.   Parents' educational level   50
Table 4.   Siblings' educational level   51
Table 5.   Informants reporting exposure to bilingual
           education or Spanish only education programs   53
Table 6.   Informants retained in school   53
Table 7.   Informants' Grade Point Averages in high
           school   55
Table 8.   Percentage of informants enrolled in Academic,
           General and Vocational curriculums while
           attending high school   55
Table 9.   Percentage of informants reporting disciplinary
           problems while attending high school   55
Table 10. Percentage of informants reporting on different
           free time activities while attending high school   56
Table 11. Percentage of informants reporting on attitudes
           toward oneself while attending high school   58
Table 12. Percentage of informants receiving support from
           parents   59
Table 13. Percentage of informants reporting first language
           skills in Spanish and English   61
Table 14. Percentage of informants reporting their English
           skills as "Excellent" or "Well"   62
Table 15. Informants reporting their Spanish skills as
           "Excellent" or "Well"   63

Table 16.   General pattern of language choice according to age difference between informant and interlocutor   65

Table 17.   Frequency totals for Language Choice for interpersonal communication   66

Table 18.   Language most favored for Receptive, Internal, Emotional and Purposeful Language   67

Table 19.   Appropriateness of language for specific topics   68

Table 20.   Means of responses to items on the *semantic differential* regarding Spanish   70

Table 21.   Percentage of informants who responded "Agree" to *affective* statements   71

Table 22.   Percentage of informants who responded "Agree" to *instrumental* items   73

Table 23.   Percentage of informants who responded "Agree" to *integrative* items   73

Table 24.   Percentage of informants who responded "Agree" to *language loyalty* items   75

Introduction

In the United States, one of the primary concerns in nearly all communities is education. Parents and community leaders seek to ensure that their children are being adequately prepared to weather the economic and intellectual challenges they will face as adults and view obtaining a high school diploma as the minimum measure by which to gauge that preparation.

Not all individuals, however, persist in school until graduating from high school. Current educational statistics reveal that on average, 12.1% of all youths and adults in the U.S. leave high school each year before completing the requirements for graduation (U.S. Department of Education 1993). Moreover, different segments of the U.S. population experience different levels of academic achievement: Hispanics[1] complete fewer years of school (10.3 years) in comparison to non-Hispanic blacks (11.9 years) or non-Hispanic whites (12.5 years) (Walker 1987).

Though estimates vary, researchers place the national dropout rate among Hispanics as the highest of any ethnic group, hovering near 45% on an annual basis (Trueba 1989, Pérez & De La Rosa Salazar 1993). Figures for urban areas, where over 85% of Hispanics reside (O'Hare 1992), are frequently much higher. Valdivieso (1986) reports that approximately 50% of Hispanics drop out of high schools in Los Angeles; in Chicago the rate is as high as 70% while New York has a Hispanic dropout rate of 80%.

The consequences for dropping out of high school are decidedly adverse. Pallas (1987) reports that dropouts are less than 50% as likely to find employment than are high school graduates and that dropouts are further disadvantaged by the limited salaries of the jobs that are available to them. The lack of employment and the low wage earnings of employed dropouts lead to billions of dollars being lost annually in federal and state tax revenue and account for additional expenditures in assistance programs (Levin 1972, Kyle et al. 1986).

More importantly however, the diminished economic means accompanying a dropout's lack of education often succeed in breeding an unfortunate legacy for subsequent generations as well. The impoverished children of parents who do not have a high school diploma are less likely to complete 12 years of school themselves, and in failing to do so, perpetuate the cycle of poverty and undereducation (Rumberger 1983, Ekstrom et al. 1987).

Besides presenting economic obstacles, a lack of education presents problems in other areas as well. Research has shown that dropouts demonstrate a lesser degree of cognitive growth in the years following their leaving school and over their lifetime, exhibit a poorer profile of health, and show a lesser degree of political participation than do students who remain in school until graduation (Pallas 1987).

In searching for answers for the high incidence of high school dropouts among Hispanic communities, political and educational policymakers have sought to identify characteristics that make Hispanics distinct from other groups. One of the most outstanding features distinguishing Hispanic communities is the retention of Spanish across generations. Currently, 71.8% of all persons of Hispanic background claim Spanish as their primary or secondary language (Solé 1990) making Hispanics the largest linguistic minority in the U.S.

Mexicans, who comprise nearly two thirds of the nation's Hispanic population, are particularly noted to have a higher cross-generational rate of retention of Spanish than any other U.S. Hispanic group (Solé 1990).[2] Furthermore, educational statistics reveal Mexicans to also be the least educated Hispanic group contributing nearly 75% of the Hispanic dropouts (U.S. Department of Education 1992c: 2-6).[3]

The coincidence of these two factors: the high dropout rates and the high degree of retention of Spanish in Hispanic, primarily Mexican, communities has erroneously prompted educational officials and the public at large to assume that the two characteristics are related. That is, there is a widespread, yet mistaken, belief that the retention of Spanish is a root cause for the lack of academic achievement among Hispanic youth. As a consequence of this false claim, "pediatricians, speech therapists, and teachers issue frightening warnings to parents, claiming that their children are cognitively confused because they are being raised bilingually…" (Zentella 1997:126). Beyond the subtle coercion of parents into eliminating non-English language interaction at home under the pretext of cognitive confusion, the misplaced emphasis on non-English languages as educational deficits, "leads policymakers and analysts to focus on language-as the 'cause' of low academic achievement, rather than considering or exploring more complex alternatives including the role of race/ethnicity, class, or discriminatory institutional practices" (Macías 1993:26). As a result, school and public officials have collaborated in perpetuating an educational institution that misguidedly assesses the academic success of Spanish-speaking children almost exclusively on the basis of their performance in English (Valdés and Figueroa 1994).

While Hispanics are more likely to drop out of school than their black or white counterparts, the complex and multiple causes for this phenomenon have not been fully explored. Until recently, studies examining the reasons behind Hispanic dropouts primarily concentrated on the sociodemographic and academic factors identified in national studies. Moreover, prior studies of Hispanics and education have not clearly focused on the relationship between academic achievement and the Spanish language. Instead, assumptions based on rates of low educational attainment or dropout have wrongly led some to conclude that the Spanish language is a barrier to educational achievement.

The goal of the present study was to explore the relationship between Spanish, English and the long-term educational outcomes of youths by examining the language use patterns and language attitude patterns of Mexican-Americans at three academic levels: High School Dropouts, High School Students and College Students. Broadly, the study sought answers to the following questions which had not been adequately addressed in previous research: Does a high degree of Spanish proficiency, Spanish use and/or the demonstration of positive attitudes toward Spanish hinder English language proficiency in the long run? Do these qualities hinder overall academic achievement? Does a high degree of English language proficiency, English language use and/or positive attitudes toward English guarantee a higher degree of academic achievement for Mexican-American youth? Do the sociodemographic and academic factors identified in national studies as contributing factors in dropping out provide valid explanations of achievement or lack of achievement among Mexican-American youth?

The primary site chosen for the study was Chicago. As Illinois' largest metropolitan area, Chicago is not only the third largest city in the U. S., but with 19.2% of the city's population being of Hispanic origin (Census of population and Housing 1993), it can also claim to be the U.S. city with the third highest number of Hispanic residents.[4] Of the city's 535,315 persons of Hispanic origin, 65% (348,040) are of Mexican descent (Census of population and Housing 1993).

The findings of the study reveal that the claim that the Spanish language is responsible for the lack of academic achievement of U.S. Mexican youths is completely unfounded. An examination of the patterns of language *use* and language *attitudes* revealed that a high use of Spanish and favorable attitudes toward Spanish *in no way* hindered either English language proficiency or long-term academic achievement among Hispanic youths. Instead, these factors were found to accompany higher levels of achievement among the Mexican-American youths surveyed. Additionally, and very much contrary to popular belief, high levels of English language proficiency, English language use, and positive attitudes toward English *were not found to guarantee high levels academic achievement.*

Moreover, several of the factors identified in national dropout studies which are considered dropout indicators were found to be prevalent among informants at all three academic levels, thus questioning the true explanatory power of such characteristics. Finally, the Mexican population of Chicago was found to exhibit different patterns of use of Spanish and English and bore different attitudes toward those languages than did Mexican populations in other parts of the U.S.

Based on these findings, we can conclude that Spanish is not a contributing factor to the high dropout rate among U.S. Mexican populations, rather, it may be that the support, development and overall confidence in Spanish language skills aided in keeping students in school. A second conclusion is that the supposed key role that English language skills and attitudes play in the academic achievement of language minority students is somewhat overrated. Students at all three levels reported having high degrees of proficiency in English and the dropouts, those who had achieved the least academically, were more likely to use English than Spanish. Finally, the fact that the Midwest Mexican informants in this study exhibited a distinct sociolinguistic profile when compared to that of Mexican populations in different parts of the country suggests that educational and sociolinguistic researchers must go beyond ethnic labels and take into consideration the particular geographic and social context and history of the population under scrutiny. In sum, instead of concentrating on unfounded assumptions, superficial characteristics, unreliable or inapplicable qualities from national studies, the policymakers and school officials who make decisions regarding Hispanic populations need to identify and focus on the characteristics that either lead to or inhibit the academic achievement of the given population in their local area.

A sense of urgency needs to be added to this admonition. Hispanics are currently one of the youngest and fastest growing subgroups of the U.S. population and are expected to be the largest minority, surpassing African-Americans, shortly after the turn of the century (O'Hare 1992, Chapa & Valencia 1993, Wright 1993). If we, as a nation, fail to appropriately and adequately address the issue of undereducation of such a large and growing segment of our population, we will have fallen short of our moral and educational obligation to Hispanic youth as well our economic obligation to all who depend on their productivity and furthermore we will place in jeopardy our position of power in the global market.

The layout of the book describing the study is as follows: Chapter 1 provides a review of the research that has identified sociodemographic and academic traits associated with dropouts and summarizes the literature that attempts to link language and academic achievement. Chapters 2 and 3 provide the statement of the problem and the methodology involved in carrying out the project. Chapter 4 presents comparative analyses of the data from each informant group, High School Dropouts, High School Students, and College Students. Finally, Chapter 5 discusses the relevant findings of the study and suggests areas for future research. The appendix at the end of the volume provides a copy of the research materials used in the study and summaries of other information relevant to the development of the research project.

NOTES

1. The term Hispanic actually encompasses a heterogeneous group of individuals whose origins lie in a variety of Indigenous, European and African races and cultures, however, because the many different peoples that come under this term share Spanish as a common heritage language, they are often wrongly assumed to be uniform in history and culture. For this reason, data are often collected on this group as a whole rather than on individual subgroups. Since the data collected by government agencies and other research entities

employ this term, it will be preserved to refer to information received from those sources. Nonetheless, in later sections, the term "Latino" will also appear with no intended variation in meaning.

2. More than half of the U.S. Hispanic population resides in the southwestern states of California and Texas, whose populations account for, respectively, 34.4% and 19.4% of U.S. Hispanic residents. The states with the next highest Hispanic populations are New York (9.9%) and Florida (7.0%) (Valdivieso 1986). Some 83% of the Hispanic residents in the Southwest are of Mexican descent (O'Hare 1992).

3. Data from the 1990 census indicate that 15.2% of Mexicans have less than a fifth grade education as opposed to 8.1% of Central or South Americans, 6.6% of Puerto Ricans, 6.5 % of Cubans and 5.2% of Hispanics of other countries of origin. Additionally, at 45.2%, Mexicans were less likely to have graduated from high school than were Puerto Ricans (60.5%), Central or South Americans (61.7%), Cubans (62.0%) or other Hispanics (70.9%) (Usdansky 1993).

4. An examination of Table 6 in O'Hare (1992) reveals that while other cities (e.g. Houston and San Antonio) have a higher percentage of residents of Hispanic origin, their total populations are considerably smaller, therefore, the actual number of Hispanic residents in each of those cities is less than the number of Hispanic residents in Chicago.

Spanish and Academic Achievement among Midwest Mexican Youth

CHAPTER 1

Language and Academic Achievement

Due to the low educational profile of U.S. Mexicans and their proclivity for retaining Spanish, language is often presumed to be a barrier to their academic success. Moreover, Spanish has often been viewed as a hindrance to the Hispanic child's cognitive development (see Hakuta 1986) and ultimately his or her access to education.[1] However, research outside the U.S. (e.g. Skutnabb-Kangas & Toukomaa 1976; Cummins 1979, 1989) has suggested that in the case of language minorities, school-provided mother tongue support (e.g. bilingual education) may aid in the development of the minority child's second language (e.g. English, here). Other research, conducted in the U.S., has suggested that programs such as bilingual education bring more than linguistic benefits to their participants by promoting success and encouraging self-esteem (Valenzuela de la Garza & Medina 1985, Huang 1990). Few studies however, have explored how Spanish may be linked to academic achievement (Díaz 1983, Hirano-Nakanishi & Díaz 1982, Hakuta & D'Andrea 1992).

Lack of English proficiency has been asserted to be a leading factor in leaving school, however "[t]he effects of oral English language proficiency on school achievement . . . have not been empirically studied to any great extent." (De Avila & Duncan 1985: 254). Updated research exploring the attitudes that underlie the patterns of use of Spanish and English (e.g. Attinasi 1985, Galindo 1991) has been lacking. Moreover, few studies have concentrated on Mexican populations outside of the Southwest (e.g. Attinasi 1985).

The present study suggests that the Mexican population in the Midwest differs from the Mexican population in the Southwest in terms of both language use and language attitudes. Furthermore, the study finds that a high degree of confidence in one's Spanish abilities and favorable attitudes toward Spanish have a positive impact upon academic achievement and that a high degree of Spanish use does not hinder academic achievement.

The following section provides an overview of the non-linguistic factors that are often cited as being associated with early school leaving among Hispanic populations. These same factors are examined across all three groups of informants in the present study.

1.1 PROFILE OF HISPANIC HIGH SCHOOL DROPOUTS

Research concerning the dropout problem has been centered on the influence of non-linguistic factors. Efforts have been made to identify the environmental variables (e.g. socioeconomic status), in-school variables (e.g. curricular track), as well as academic traits (e.g. grade point average), and student behaviors (e.g. truancy). However, research has revealed the problem is complex and associated with a variety of factors and not wholly attributable to any single one (cf. Bachman, Green and Wirtanen 1971; Bachman, O'Malley and Johnson 1971; Rock et al. 1986; Ekstrom et al. 1987).

One of the more recent comprehensive longitudinal studies on high school achievement was the High School and Beyond (HS & B) project. In its initial year (1980) the project involved approximately 30,000 high school sophomores and 28,000 high school seniors attending some one thousand private and public high schools. The project was to continue surveying and testing students and dropouts every two years for a decade Valdivieso (1986).[2] Many researchers have used the information provided in the HS & B database to identify the student background and behaviors as well as the school characteristics that were most strongly associated with dropping out in general (e.g. Ekstrom et al. 1987) and with particular reference to Hispanic populations (e.g. Valdivieso 1986, Hirano-Nakanishi 1986). Results from these studies as well as other research on Hispanic dropouts will be presented in the sections that follow.

1.1.1 Social characteristics

The most salient characteristics consistently associated with dropout are race/ethnicity and socioeconomic status (SES). Blacks are more likely to drop out than are non-Hispanic whites, and individuals of Hispanic origin are more likely to drop out than blacks (Bachman, Green and Wirtanen 1971; Bachman, O'Malley and Johnson 1971; Rock et al. 1986; Ekstrom et al. 1987).[3] With regard to SES, students from a more impoverished environment are more prone to drop out than more affluent students.[4]

Other factors associated with dropping out identified by Ekstrom et al. (1987) are: living in an urban setting, coming from large, single-mother-headed families, and having parents and/or siblings who themselves had not completed high school. Valverde (1986) identified a connection between immigrant status and dropping out among Hispanics, finding that the dropouts in her study were more likely to be U.S. born, while Hispanics who had been born abroad were more likely to succeed in obtaining their high school diploma. Similarly, Cuban (1989) suggested that "immigrants persist in school longer and have stronger overall academic records than non-immigrant youths . . . " (p. 126).

Many of the characteristics associated with dropping out of high school are traits that are prevalent in many Hispanic communities.[5] Census data from 1980 indicate that at least four out of every five Hispanics live in a metropolitan setting (U.S. House of Representatives 1983, Valdivieso 1986). Data from the 1990 Census show that Hispanic families, with 3.48 persons per household, are larger on average than non-Hispanic families who have an average of 2.58 persons per household.[6] Social scientists estimate that for families of any race, each additional child raises the odds of any child in that family dropping out by 8% (Hauser and Phang 1993:28).

U.S. Hispanics also comprise the poorest segment of the nation's population. Hispanic workers, on average, are least compensated for their labor when compared to persons of other racial or ethnic backgrounds, and Hispanic women are the worst paid overall.[7] Moreover, 1990 Census data indicate that Hispanic households rely on the earnings of a single parent, often a mother, twice as often as non-Hispanic white households (Usdansky 1993).[8] Annually, Hispanic households earn $8,000 to $10,000 less than non-Hispanic households.[9] It is not surprising then to find that more Hispanic families live under the poverty level (28.7%) than do all non-Hispanics (12.8%) or non-Hispanic whites (9.4%) (Usdansky 1993). Adding further strain to Hispanics' weak economic base is the fact that Hispanic parents are less likely to possess a high school diploma,[10] meaning that they are less eligible for more highly skilled, better paying jobs.[11]

Despite their lower earning potential, Hispanics in general are more likely to respond to economic distress with work than through dependence on social welfare programs than are other minority groups.[12] However, placing an excessive emphasis on employment while in high school may serve to encourage students to drop out. Researchers note that limited part-time employment may be beneficial for high school students, however, working in excess of 15 hours per week often has a negative impact on a high school student's academic attainment.[13]

Nonetheless, Hispanic students exhibit a strong work ethic. Lewin-Epstein (1981) found that Hispanic high school seniors in the 1980 HS & B database had higher labor participation rates, worked for more hours than any other racial/ethnic group, and were more likely than any other group to hold a full time job while attending school.[14] Moreover, Valdivieso (1986) found that Hispanic dropouts were nearly twice as likely as non-Hispanic white students to report having left high school to work and support their family. Current estimates indicate that nearly one-fourth of Hispanic high school students are working while attending school and more than half of these students are working in excess of 20 hours per week (U.S. Department of Education 1992a:120). Still, the fact that the dropout rate exceeds the labor rate of Hispanic youths by a considerable amount indicates that working while in high school might be a concomitant factor in the high rate of Hispanic dropouts rather than being a primary influence in a Hispanic's decision to leave school before completing a diploma.

Likewise, while low socioeconomic status might be expected to be a reasonable explanation for the excessive dropout problem of Hispanic youth, previous studies have produced contradictory conclusions, suggesting that this factor also does not fully account for the high rate of leaving school. Within the Hispanic community, Hirano-Nakanishi (1986) found that poor Hispanics left school between two and five times more often than did less disadvantaged Hispanics. Valverde (1986), however, found that the family backgrounds of both Hispanic dropouts and graduates were on par with one another economically as well as educationally. Examining the effects of SES cross-culturally,

Steinberg, Blinde, and Chan (1984) found that even when SES is held constant, Latino students are still 1.5 to 3 times more likely to dropout than non-Hispanic whites. Similarly, Rumberger (1983) found disadvantaged Hispanics dropped out at rates 40-50% higher than poor non-Hispanic blacks. Additionally, Steinberg, Blinde, and Chan (1984) found that when family factors such as the number of parents and siblings are controlled, Hispanics still tend to drop out at higher rates than do individuals of other ethnic groups.[15] Thus, rather than fully explaining the Hispanic dropout problem, the social background characteristics prevalent in the Hispanic community may work in conjunction with other factors particular to Hispanic youths to contribute to early school leaving.

1.1.2 Educational achievement

While sociodemographic factors such as race/ethnicity and SES are consistently associated with leaving school early, dropping out is also often associated with elements of school achievement, student attitudes and student behaviors while attending high school. Dropouts, more so than graduates, report receiving low grades (Bachman, Green and Wirtanen 1971, Ekstrom et al. 1987).[16] Pallas (1987) confirms that receiving poor grades is one of the best indicators of dropouts in reference to Hispanic high school students. Durán (1983) noted that grade point averages for Hispanics are, for the most part, lower than for non-Hispanic white students.[17] Similarly, Valdivieso (1986) found that roughly one-third of the male and one-third of the female Hispanic dropouts reported that receiving low grades in school influenced their decision to dropout.

Dropouts are also more likely to have been retained in a grade one or more years (Orum 1985, Ekstrom et al. 1987). A direct result of grade retention is what is often termed the "overage phenomenon". This refers to the situation created when the students who have been retained find themselves repeating a class with peers who are younger than they are; an age gap that widens with each subsequent retention. Orum (1985) and Ekstrom et al. (1987) have already identified the influence that being older than one's class peers has on dropping out. Research has shown that this influence is particularly pronounced among Hispanic youth (Hirano-Nakanishi 1986, Valdivieso 1986, Vélez 1989). In particular, Hirano-Nakanishi (1986) revealed that nearly 40% of all Hispanic dropouts leave school before their sophomore year of high school. The researcher concluded that leaving school early may be encouraged by retention not only by compounding a sense of academic failure and exaggerating the age gap between the retained student and his/her class peers, but also by providing a legal exit from school at an earlier grade (age 16 in most states).[18]

Due to a perceived lackluster performance exhibited in earlier grades, Hispanic students who do reach high school are placed ("tracked"), more often than not, in less academically challenging curriculums that place a higher emphasis on appropriate public conduct than on critical thinking.[19] Moreover, high school seniors of Mexican descent have been found to be the Hispanic subgroup least likely to be enrolled in an academic curriculum (O'Malley 1987: 27). Similarly, Valdivieso (1986) noted that three-quarters of all Latino students were not enrolled in college preparatory curriculums and that furthermore, the vast majority of students in these tracks reported getting lower than average grades. Moreover, the researcher discovered that the majority (92%) of Hispanic dropouts in the HS & B database had been enrolled in the general and vocational tracks meaning that a minority (8%) had dropped out from a college preparatory curriculum.

The effects of low grades, retention, being overage and placement in a less challenging curricular track quickly compound and can affect a student's attitudes and behaviors. Bachman, Green and Wirtanen (1971) and Ekstrom et al. (1987) have found that dropouts report a higher degree of dissatisfaction with school and express a lower degree of self-esteem. These researchers also found that dropouts have higher instances of disciplinary problems (e.g. suspension) and exhibit lower attendance rates. Additionally, dropouts in these studies devoted less time to homework and rarely participated in school-sponsored extracurricular activities. Finally, these researchers noted that dropouts were less likely to feel in control of their own destiny and would more often attribute their dissatisfaction and lack of success to external forces such as "bad luck" or "other people" who were holding them back (Bachman, Green and Wirtanen 1971, Ekstrom et al 1987).

Valdivieso (1986) found similar traits among Hispanic dropouts, however, he noted that Hispanics reported being dissatisfied with school less often than their non-Hispanic white peers. Non-Hispanic blacks also reported more dissatisfaction with school than did Hispanics, but less than non-Hispanic whites (Rumberger 1983) suggesting that dropping out due to not liking school may be culturally bound.

Marriage and pregnancy are often cited by Hispanic and non-Hispanic white and non-Hispanic black females as strong factors influencing their decision to leave school (Rumberger 1983, Valdivieso 1986, Ekstrom et al. 1987), while both Hispanic and non-Hispanic white males frequently report leaving school to work (Valdivieso 1986). Kyle (1989) and Reyes and Jason (1993), researching the schools in the Chicago area, have suggested that gangs and the threat they present to personal safety may also influence students' decisions to leave school.

In addition to the student behaviors and attitudes mentioned above, Ekstrom et al. (1987) attributed an important role of a child's academic success to his/her parents. Parents of dropouts in the study were not found to be likely to provide assistance with homework and were not known to engage their children in discussions about their post-high school plans. The same study also reported that parents of dropouts were frequently unaware of where to locate their children during non-school hours.

1.1.3 Sociolinguistic characteristics

While Hispanics bear the burden of socioeconomic and academic traits that hinder academic progress to a disproportionate degree, Steinberg, Blinde, and Chan (1984) suggest that these factors do not fully explain the high rate of school leaving among Hispanics.   Many researchers contend that the pervasive nature of Spanish within the Hispanic community, the recency of immigration of many Hispanics as well as the young age of the Hispanic population (see Introduction) have an impact on a large proportion of school-aged Latino youths. Chapa and Valencia (1993) note that these three factors mean that two-thirds of Latino school children are challenged by ". . . differences between the language and culture of the United States and a foreign country . . . they were first exposed to a foreign language and culture through their own experience or through their immigrant parent or parents." (p. 174) Nonetheless, studies have yet to consider how language background, independent of social and economic characteristics, affects Hispanic dropout rates (Steinberg, Blinde, and Chan 1984).

Linguistic minorities, that is, ethnic minorities that have retained the use of a non-English language, have often been classified in educational contexts as being "disadvantaged," and their non-English background has been seen as a "barrier" to full access to educational opportunities (cf. footnote 1). To wit, language minority status has been identified as a strong predictor of grade retention (Durán 1983, Steinberg, Blinde and Chan 1984).

Data from the National Center for Educational Statistics confirm this notion. One report, using data from 1989, indicates that while 34.7% of all children aged 8-15 were at least one year behind their normal grade, 39.9% of children who reported speaking Spanish at home were behind one year or more (U.S. Department of Education 1992a: 22).[20] The same report indicates that while 37.7% of all Low English Proficient (LEP) students have been retained at least one year, 42.1% of Spanish-speaking LEP students have been held back, compared to only 32.8% of speakers of other languages.[21] While LEP status is usually determined by school officials, Hispanics students' judgements about their own English proficiency has also been positively correlated with high school achievement (Nielsen and Fernández 1981).

Although linguistic minorities in general appear to be behind their monolingual English peers, it seems that persons from a Spanish speaking background are disproportionately disadvantaged. Veltman (1980) examined different racial/ethnic and linguistic groups ranging in ages from 6 to 17 to determine what influence language usage might play in predicting educational attainment.[22] Spanish-speaking Hispanic youths demonstrated below average levels of attainment. However, youths who spoke other non-English languages or children who reported having one or more parents speak another language at home tended to display above average levels of educational attainment. The researcher concluded that due to the wide fluctuation in attainment between speakers of different non-English backgrounds, there were not sufficient grounds to suggest language minority status as a causal factor in a child's educational attainment.

Even more compelling was Veltman's finding that not only were Spanish-speaking Hispanic children found to have the lowest levels of educational attainment over all groups examined (non-Hispanic blacks, non-Hispanic whites, and English-speaking Hispanics), but the Spanish-speaking youths aged 14-17, were the only group that demonstrated a *negative* mean of educational attainment. That is, while Spanish-speaking Hispanics were initially at a disadvantage displaying less educational attainment than the age peers of other races and language backgrounds to whom they were being compared, Spanish-speaking Hispanics had actually regressed to a position even further behind the other groups as they increased in age (Veltman 1980:Table 1). These findings suggest that being from a linguistic minority background may in some cases place students at a disadvantage. However, Veltman's (1980) results more clearly demonstrate a disparity between being from a Spanish-speaking background as opposed to being from language minority background that is not Spanish and suggest that further research into the relationship between a Spanish-language background and academic achievement is warranted.

Further evidence which appears to link a Spanish language background to dropping out has been revealed in other studies. Bilingual and monolingual Spanish speaking Hispanics between the ages of 14 and 30 were found to be 2.5 times as likely to have dropped out of school than their non-Hispanic white peers, while monolingual English speaking Hispanics were seen to be on par with English-speaking non-Hispanic whites (U.S. House of Representatives 1983).[23] Additionally, non-English speaking Hispanics were found to have higher rates of pre-high school attrition than were English speaking Hispanics (Hirano-Nakanishi 1986). More recently, it has been noted that Hispanics who speak Spanish at home and don't speak English at all (i.e. monolinguals) dropped out at a rate of more than 83% ("Language woes" 1994).

In general, these studies point to a negative influence on the part of Spanish, but do not provide empirical evidence that Spanish is at the root of diminished academic achievement among Latinos. Moreover, these studies provide evidence of a positive link between minority languages and academic achievement.

Skutnabb-Kangas & Toukomaa (1976) and Cummins (1979, 1989) have shown positive linguistic and academic benefits associated with the early development of a linguistic minorities' mother tongue. Likewise, Curiel, Rosenthal and Richek (1986) found that Mexican youths in Houston who were exposed to bilingual education programs were retained less often and were less likely to drop out when compared to those who had not had bilingual education. Additionally, the researchers noted a correlation between grade point average and length of participation in the bilingual program; higher grades were associated with a greater length of exposure to bilingual education. Similar results were reported for Mexican youths in Tucson (Valenzuela de la Garza & Medina 1985).

Lacking in all of the studies in the literature in general, however, is an examination of how Spanish proficiency and the degree of Spanish use affect academic achievement. Preliminary explorations of these topics have produced mixed results. Nielsen and Fernández (1981) found that while Spanish proficiency was positively correlated with Hispanics' scores on achievement measures, actual Spanish use had a negative influence. That is, while a greater knowledge of Spanish aided English test performance, a higher degree of usage of Spanish with family members appeared to be detrimental.[24] On the other hand, Ortiz (1989) examined the literacy rates of Hispanic young adults between the ages of 21 and 25 and found that neither Spanish proficiency nor the frequency of use of Spanish had any bearing on literacy skills. López (1982) found that populations that maintained a high use of Spanish exhibited two separate trends; one which was characterized by low levels of income, education, and employment status; and another that reflected high academic achievement.

Additionally lacking is research relating the attitudes of language minorities toward their heritage language and academic achievement. Given that the Spanish language and ethnic identity are so closely linked in Mexican-American culture (Trueba 1989), the attitudes expressed by Latinos toward Spanish (and English) may signify a reflection of one's self-esteem (Galindo 1991) and/or tendency toward assimilation (Hurtado & Gurín 1987). While positive attitudes may not accurately reflect use due to situational circumstances (Hakuta & D'Andrea 1992), negative attitudes expressed toward a minority language may serve to alter their use in subsequent generations (Galindo 1991). In sum,

> Unless we probe deeper into the process of Spanish-language maintenance by way of considering attitudinal, affective and motivational factors in addition to sociodemographic configurations, we may not understand why Hispanics are experiencing currently a more retentive linguistic profile than other non-English mother-tongue groups in the United States . . . Solé (1985: 296)

While studies such as Elías-Olivares (1976b), Suárez-Orozco (1987) and others examine language as a means of cultural transmission, they do not relate these issues to academic achievement. A search revealed only one study, Watt et al. (1992), which examined cultural attachment (including language) and academic achievement.

These researchers found that close ties to Spanish and Mexican culture neither aided nor hindered Mexican-American academic achievement. Thus, the relationship between Hispanic academic achievement and use of and attitudes toward Spanish and English are issues that must be further explored.

1.2 SOCIOLINGUISTIC PROFILE OF THE MEXICAN COMMUNITY

Before researching the language use and language attitudes of the Spanish speaking Mexican community in Chicago, it is useful to briefly examine the social history of Mexicans in the U.S. By providing an historical context, we can gain insight into the experiences that have shaped the language attitudes and language use patterns of the country's largest linguistic minority (St. Clair 1982).

1.2.1 Social profile

The Mexican descendants are, by far, the Spanish speaking people that can trace their roots back the farthest on the North American continent. In the late 16th century, Mexicans and their Spanish ancestors colonized what is now known as the Southwest United States. Some 250 years later, as a result of two years of military conflict with the United States, Mexico ceded more than half of its territory in the Treaty of Guadalupe Hidalgo in 1848. The Mexicans who at that time lived in the areas now known as Texas, New Mexico, Arizona, Colorado, Nevada, Utah, California and parts of Oklahoma and Wyoming became U.S. residents not because they had crossed over the border, but rather because the border had crossed over *them!* (Ford Foundation 1984; Griswold del Castillo 1990:9)

The exponential growth experienced by the Mexican population in the Southwest was not gained without struggle. Many of the later immigrants came from rural areas of Mexico, were of scarce economic means and were often only marginally literate. Their mother country was economically strapped and fraught with internal conflict. Even so, the U.S. proved to be less than charitable.

While initially tolerant of the Mexican culture and language, many Southwest states later enacted pro-English policies that discriminated against Mexicans and their language and excluded them from the political process (Kanellos 1993). Over the course of time, this history marked by intolerance and outright prejudice has engendered an image of Mexicans as lower class, poor, and intellectually inferior.

Although U.S. Mexicans and their descendants espouse a link to a common background, there are several factors that have influenced their linguistic experiences over time. First, the multigenerational nature of the U.S. Mexican population is an important consideration. The fact that many families can trace their roots to five generations or more in the U.S. while other families are more recently arrived provides for a broad spectrum of linguistic variety (López 1982).[25] Moreover, while the use of immigrant languages in the U.S. normally declines with each subsequent generation and is often nearly extinct by the third generation (Fishman et al. 1966, Fishman 1973, Veltman 1983), decline in the use of Spanish occurs at a much slower rate than for other minority languages and has been noted to be retained to a higher degree than other immigrant languages through the third generation (López 1982, Veltman 1983). Additionally, of all U.S. Latino populations, Mexicans have proven to be the most persistent in retaining Spanish (López 1987, 1982; Veltman 1983; Solé 1985, 1990).[26]

The proximity of Mexico to the United States and the ties that U.S. Mexicans retain with their heritage country also influence linguistic patterns. The geographical position of Mexico provides not only a constant influx of new immigrants, but also allows ample opportunity for U.S. residents to remain in contact with family members south of the border. This flow is not hampered by the additional distance Mexican immigrants must travel to reach beyond the Southwest; Solé (1990: Table 6) reports that 44.4% of the Mexicans residing in Illinois are foreign born.

The geographical concentration of Hispanics, and of Mexican-descended individuals in particular, within the United States may influence their linguistic behaviors and beliefs (Solé 1990, Galindo 1991). Mexicans and their descendents account for nearly two-thirds of U.S. Hispanics (U.S. Department of Education 1992c, O'Hare 1992), the majority of whom reside in the Southwest. Some 61% of the population in the southwestern states is of Hispanic origin with the populations of California and Texas accounting for more than 50% of the nation's Hispanic population (O'Hare 1992). Of the Hispanics in the Southwest, 83% are of Mexican origin (O'Hare 1992). High populations of Mexicans and their descendents are also found clustered in the Midwest.

The city of Chicago, for example, is home to the third largest urban Hispanic community in the U.S. (O'Hare 1992). Currently residing in the Chicago area are some 535,315 persons of Hispanic origin, representing 19.2% of the city's population of slightly over 2.2 million and some 65% (348,040) of Chicago's Hispanics are of Mexican descent (Census of Population and Housing 1993). Moreover, of Chicago Hispanics over the age of five, 446,598 (83%) report speaking Spanish, underscoring the notion that Spanish is still a vital element in the daily interaction of the Midwest Hispanic population (Census of population and Housing 1993).

The ethnic concentration of the Spanish speakers and recency of immigration of many of the Mexicans in the Chicago area affect their linguistic attitudes and language use. As will be seen in the following two sections of this chapter, however, little sociolinguistic research has been conducted in this area.

1.2.2 Language use

Research on the language use patterns of Mexican descended speakers has revealed that the use of Spanish and English are often guided by the formality of the situation. In the Southwest, Spanish has been found to be preferred for use in the home (Carranza and Ryan 1975), and in cultural, religious, and intragroup interactions (Barker 1972, Solé 1976, Galindo 1991).

Barker (1972) found that Spanish was also used as an intragroup means of communication, employed exclusively for interactions between members of the Spanish speaking community. Despite a demonstrated proficiency in Spanish, Barker found Spanish speakers in Tucson reluctant to engage Anglos in a conversation in Spanish. He also discovered that a more formal variety of Spanish was used during public meetings and religious ceremonies while a more colloquial variety was used in a family setting. More recent findings indicate that U.S. born Mexican youths in Texas still utilize Spanish in domains of household, church, neighborhood and local businesses (Galindo 1991).

English, on the other hand, was found to be used for interaction on a more formal level among Mexican descended communities. Carranza & Ryan (1975) revealed a preference for using English at school, while Solé (1976) found that English was not only used for academic topics, but for political, technical or occupational topics also.

Age of both the speaker and interlocutor exerts an influence over the use of Spanish or English in conversations. Researchers of Mexican populations have found that older generations tend to interact and are interacted with more in Spanish, while speakers of younger generations tended toward bilingualism (e.g. Skrabanek 1970, Thompson 1974, Attinasi 1985, Floyd 1985, Solé 1985, Galindo 1991).[27] Similarly, Laosa (1975) noted that while language patterns differed among generations within individual Mexican-American families, the language parents reported using most frequently was reflected in the language that their children used most frequently.[28]

Attinasi (1985) compared the language choice of Mexican and Puerto Rican populations in the Gary, Indiana area with that of Puerto Rican residents of New York.[29] The researcher's Gary sample tended to use a higher degree of English when socializing and generally showed a trend toward a shift to English.[30] Nonetheless, informants in the Gary sample reported speaking in Spanish or alternating between languages (using either Spanish or English) more often than the New York informants on some of the measures, suggesting that for the moment, Spanish still remains an integral part of social life in the Midwest. Moreover, Solé (1990) reports that 50.9% of Hispanic preschoolers in Illinois are incipient bilinguals (i.e. they are more dominant in Spanish than in English) or are Spanish monolinguals. From these results she concludes that Spanish is most likely the primary language of the household.

Linguistic behavior, however, does not necessarily govern an individual's attitudes toward a language, nor do language attitudes necessarily reflect language use.[31] Nonetheless, an examination of the attitudes a bilingual holds toward the languages s/he speaks in combination with an exploration of the patterns of language use can provide insight into the motivations behind the bilingual's choice of using (or not using) a language.

1.2.3 Language attitudes

Research on the beliefs and behaviors of Spanish speaking communities has taken many forms. Studies have examined specific Hispanic communities,[32] other studies have described the forms and uses of particular varieties of Spanish[33] and described the reactions to different language varieties.[34] While the literature is vast in scope and definition (see Agheyisi and Fishman 1970, and Cooper and Fishman

1974), the present review will limit its examination to *affective, integrative* and *instrumental* orientations and feelings of *language loyalty* following Cooper and Fishman's (1974, 1977) definitions.

An *affective* attitude refers to the pleasurable feelings one has toward, or personal satisfaction one derives from being associated with an object, in this case a language (Cooper and Fishman 1974). An *affective* attitude is often seen in individuals such as Hannum's (1978) Mexican-American college informants who claimed that maintenance of Spanish was important primarily for personal fulfillment. Likewise, Adorno's (1973) Mexican parental informants felt that their children should develop skills in Spanish primarily for idealistic rather than practical reasons.

Similarly, an *integrative* attitude refers to an individual's desire to associate with a given group as defined by some common background feature. A strong *integrative* association with Spanish has long been established in the Mexican and Mexican-American community. Spanish has been seen as an expression of unity and solidarity (Ayer 1969, Solé 1976, Weller 1983),[35] as well as a vehicle through which a community can rediscover its lost roots (Cisneros & Leone 1983). Mexican and Mexican-American speakers have also been known to define their cultural identity through speaking Spanish (Ramírez 1974, Carranza & Ryan 1975, LaTouche 1976, Ryan & Carranza 1977) or through code-switching (Elías-Olivares 1976a, 1976b).

Feelings of *language loyalty* reflect a linguistic minority's desire to retain a less privileged language, in spite of the possible negative social and economic consequences they might face by doing so (Cooper and Fishman 1977). The high degree of *language loyalty* toward Spanish among Mexican communities can be seen through the retention of Spanish across generations as seen previously (e.g. Thompson 1974, López 1982). Informants in some studies have expressed a desire to maintain Spanish in order to perpetuate the language's link with the culture of the community (Solé 1976, Hannum 1978, Galindo 1991).[36]

An *instrumental* orientation refers to an individual's desire to associate with a given group based on the social and/or economic benefits derived from doing so. Galindo asserts that the minority and majority languages in bilingual communities compete such that ". . . upward mobility of an ethnic minority is linked with language shift to the dominant language" (1991:15).

For Southwest Spanish speakers of Mexican descent, Spanish does not have an *instrumental* value; i.e. Spanish is not associated with social or economic benefits. Studies have found that Mexicans in poorer conditions express more negative feelings toward Spanish than those in a more stable economic situation, who express more positive views (Grebler et al. 1970, Elías-Olivares 1976). English, on the other hand, has been shown to have *instrumental* value for Mexican communities. Grebler et al. (1970) and Elías-Olivares (1976a) found that respondents readily associated English with social mobility. English, however, has not been seen to be associated with *integrative* or *affective* attitudes among Spanish speaking communities.

Research concerning language use patterns of Mexicans has primarily focused attention on communities in the Southwest. Elías-Olivares (1995), who examined the discourse strategies of Mexicans in Chicago and Farr and Guerra (1995) who examined the levels of literacy of Mexicans in the same city are recent and notable exceptions. Hutchinson (1990) examined the language use patterns of various Latino communities in Chicago. He reports that among Mexicans, Spanish was most likely to be used when speaking to relatives, particularly spouses, but was least likely to be used by children when speaking among themselves. Hutchinson concludes that a rapid shift to English will occur despite the constant influx of Latino immigrants drawn the city's industries.

There is a similar lack of research regarding the language attitudes of Midwest Mexican populations. However, in light of Attinasi's (1985) Gary respondents, who as a whole expressed favorable attitudes toward Spanish, but 78.5% of whom *did not feel* that Spanish constituted an essential element of Latino culture, it is evident that research on Mexican's attitudes toward Spanish need to be further explored in other regions.

At present, two principle factors have been observed as prevalent in U.S. Mexican communities: 1) a high degree of retention of Spanish, and 2) low levels of academic achievement. The concurrence of these two characteristics has often led educators and policymakers to make the assumption, without more than anecdotal evidence as a foundation, that the former factor is to blame for the latter. However, the validity of such a claim can only truly be tested by evaluating the sociolinguistic and academic characteristics of the population in question. The present study is born out of the need to provide solid evidence regarding the relationship between the use of Spanish and English and the academic achievement of youths of Mexican descent.

Furthermore, previous studies demonstrate that U.S. Mexican populations from different regions of the country differ with respect to their use of Spanish and English and their attitudes toward both languages. The present study then, will add to the small body of research regarding the sociolinguistic profile of Mexican-American populations outside of the Southwest.

NOTES

1. This assumption is evident in a government-commissioned summary of the U.S. Hispanic population. The authors of a section regarding education opened with the statement "Due in part to the language barrier, Hispanics face a hurdle to an appropriate education." (U.S. House of Representatives 1983:18)

2. This project was undertaken as part of the National Center for Educational Statistics' (NCES) Study of Excellence in High School Education (cf. Rock et al. 1986). Initial HS & B data was derived from surveys and achievement tests administered to participants. Two years later over 22,000 of the 1980 sophomores were resurveyed and retested during their senior year in high school. Additionally, data was collected from over 2000 of the 1980 sophomores that had dropped out by 1982.

3. Data from the U.S. Department of Education (1992a: 58) reveal that by age 20, 12.7% of non-Hispanic white students, 22.4% of non-Hispanic black students and 40.3% of Hispanic students still do not possess a high school diploma

4. For more complete summaries of general dropout characteristics, see Bachman, Green & Wirtanen (1971), Bachman, O'Malley & Johnson, (1971), Rock et al. (1986), Ekstrom et al. (1987); for studies related specifically to Hispanic dropouts, see Hirano-Nakanishi (1986), Valdivieso (1986) and Vélez (1989).

5. Cubans, for reasons related to the circumstances surrounding their immigration to the U.S., differ from other U.S. Hispanic populations in terms of their educational and socioeconomic status (Durán 1983).

6. Of all of the Hispanic subgroups, Mexicans, with an average of 3.84 persons, have the largest families (Wright 1993: 282).

7. Labor statistics from the 3rd quarter of 1990 indicate that Hispanic men earn a weekly average of $317, slightly higher than the $302 reported weekly earnings for Hispanic women. Average weekly salaries for black males and females were higher or equal to that of Hispanics ($438 and $302, respectively), but still short of the reported average weekly earnings for white males ($492) or females ($350) (Kanellos 1993: 350).

8. 1990 census data indicate that nearly 32% of Hispanic households are headed by a single parent and that nearly three-quarters of Hispanic single parents are women. In contrast, only 21% of black households and 16% of white households are run by one parent (Usdansky 1993).

9. Hispanic households were shown to earn an annual average of $22,688; considerably less than the average $30,706 for all non-Hispanics or the average $32,311 for white non-Hispanics (Usdansky 1993).

10. During the period between 1973 and 1989, the mean years of schooling for heads of households increased considerably for non-Hispanic blacks (from 9.5 to 11.5 years) as well as for non-Hispanic whites (from 12 years to 13 years), while Hispanic heads of house showed a much less degree of increase in average years of schooling over the same period (from 9 years to 9.5 years) (Hauser and Phang 1993).

11. Usdansky (1993) reveals that only 52.6% of all Hispanics aged 25 years or older had at least completed their high school diploma compared with 81.5% of similarly aged non-Hispanics.

12. U.S. House of Representatives (1983: 58) reports that in 1980, Hispanic labor force participation was at 64.0%, comparable to the rate for all workers (63.8%). In the 1990 census, Hispanics were revealed to be less dependent on welfare programs than were Native American or African-American families (O'Hare 1992: Table 11)

13. Steinberg, Greenberger, Garduque and McAuliffe (1982) noted that limited part time employment accompanies slight increases in students' grades. However, these researchers and others found that when high school students work exceeded 15 hours per week, their attendance rates, satisfaction with school and grades all dropped. Other researchers have noted that when high schoolers work between 15 and 21 hours per week, their chance of dropping out increases by 50%; when students work more than 22 hours per week, their likelihood of dropping out is doubled (Barro 1984, Pallas 1984, D'Amico 1984).

14. Moreover, it was found that while the Latino student's wages were lower in actual dollars, their salaries accounted for a higher percentage of their family's income.

15. Rumberger's (1983) analysis did not find any increase in Hispanic dropout rates when these factors were controlled.

16. In addition to grades, many of the studies investigating the dropout phenomenon have noted that dropouts often score poorly on standardized achievement measures of verbal and mathematical ability (Bachman, Green & Wirtanen 1971, Ekstrom et al. 1987). Though such assessment is beyond the scope of this project, it should be noted that research has found that Hispanic

students' scores on such measures consistently lag behind those of other ethnic groups (Veltman 1980, O'Malley 1987).

17. Similar statistics regarding the average grades for non-Hispanic blacks were not available.

18. However, counterevidence to this trend is provided by Hauser and Phang (1993) who note that percentage of 18 and 19 year olds that have not completed at least eight years of school has not risen above 5% over the last two decades for Hispanics, non-Hispanic blacks and non-Hispanic whites. Furthermore, these researchers present data that suggest that for all three of these racial/ethnic groups, dropout rates increase with each successive grade in school, i.e. higher percentages of 11th graders drop out than 10th graders and higher percentages of 12th graders dropout than 11 graders. (Hauser and Phang 1993: Table 1).

19. Criticism of this practice as discriminatory against minorities has been raised by Oakes (1985) who notes that minorities and disadvantaged youth are disproportionately assigned to non-academic curriculums in which instructors expect less from the students and devote less time to developing critical thinking skills and more time to shaping the students' behavior, ultimately limiting the students' post-secondary opportunities. Likewise, Rosenbaum (1976, 1980) found that school officials provide students in college bound tracks with more thorough information than students in non-college tracks. As a result, students in general and vocational tracks are often not eligible for college admission because of inadequate academic preparation.

20. Only 26.7% of those who spoke all other European languages, 28.0% of those who spoke Asian languages and 35.2% of those who spoke any other language in their home were held back as often.

21. The 32.8% reported represents Asian language speakers only; data on other LEP linguistic minorities was too scarce to be reliable.

22. Educational attainment was defined as appropriate grade placement according to age.

23. The authors of the report state that the low graduation rates of non-monolingual English Hispanics ". . . does not necessarily imply that background in a language other than English is the specific or sole cause of high non-completion rates. Rather, it indicates that a non-English background may relate to degree of assimilation, facility in English, or to socioeconomic conditions impacting on the likelihood of completing school." (U.S. House of Representatives 1983:26)

24. However, this may only hold true for certain Hispanic subgroups. Durán (1983) reports that though Cuban-American communities maintain a high

degree of Spanish use this does not appear to hinder their educational achievement.

25. Much research has been devoted to the linguistic description and sociolinguistic contextualization of different varieties of Spanish, however, such topics are beyond the scope of the present study. Nonetheless, Ornstein (1970) Teschner, Bills & Craddock (1975), and Hernández-Chávez, Cohen and Beltramo (1975) provide information regarding earlier work while Peñalosa (1980, 1981) and Elías-Olivares (1983), and Veltman (1988), present more recent research.

26. Mexican-American populations in particular have been noted to utilize Spanish at a rate of 98% for the first generation and 34% for the second generation. By the third generation, the rate of Spanish use had dropped to 16% (López 1978). Non-Spanish speaking linguistic minority groups are considerably more anglicized (Veltman 1983).

27. Extensive documentation exists regarding the generational trend of Spanish speakers in general toward using both Spanish and English (López 1978, Veltman 1983) and Mexican populations in particular (Floyd 1985, Galindo 1991).

28. Parents who spoke English most frequently in the home had children that did the same; parents speaking Spanish most frequently in the home had the children who code-switched most. Children code-switched least when their parents used Spanish and English equally, but children were most likely to code-mix if their parents also did so. More detail on code-switching patterns can be found in Wentz & McClure (1975), McClure (1977), Poplack (1982) and Silva-Corvalán (1983).

29. Due to its small size, the Gary sample was not delineated on cultural lines, therefore, there is no accurate assessment of how the responses of Mexican informants may have differed from those of the Midwest Puerto Rican informants.

30. Attinasi suggested that this may have been due to the fact that the Gary sample's friendships were more cross-cultural than those of the New York informants and that this may have had an impact on their use of Spanish and English.

31. For example, regarding languages in addition to one's mother tongue Fishman states, "On the whole, English . . . is more learned than used and more used than liked. The three (learning, using, and liking) are little related to each other" (1977:126). Hakuta and D'Andrea (1992) note, however, that a bilingual may hold positive attitudes toward his or her heritage language, but may be constrained in its use by circumstances of work or school.

32. See Fishman, Cooper & Ma (1971) for an extensive review of Spanish in the New York Puerto Rican community, García et al. (1988) for New York Dominicans.

33. For Mexican-American varieties of Spanish in the Southwest see Ornstein (1970), Hernández-Chávez, Cohen and Beltramo (1975), Elías-Olivares (1976a, 1976b, 1983), Peñalosa (1980, 1981), Aguirre (1982, 1984), Hart-González and Feingold (1990) and Galindo (1991). Teschner, Bills & Craddock (1975) provide an annotated bibliography of overall linguistic research of U.S. Hispanic communities.

34. A considerable body of work has been done concerning the reactions to accented or non-standard dialects of English and Spanish. Cohen (1974) examined parents' attitudes as to where the "best" Spanish was spoken, Amastae and Elías-Olivares (1978) and Ryan and Carranza (1977) examined reactions to Southwest varieties of Spanish, while Carranza (1982) presents a summary of findings regarding Latino language attitudes toward both English and Spanish. Gynan (1985) examines reactions to both native and non-native Spanish. Giles, et al. (1995) explore reactions to Anglo- and Hispanic-accented English.

35. Weller's (1983) study did not reflect solely the attitudes of Mexicans, rather examined the small, cosmopolitan community of Spanish speakers in Washington, D.C.

36. Solé writes, "Spanish is viewed as a link with and symbol of the Hispanic heritage, and language maintenance is considered essential if cultural continuity is to be preserved for oneself and future generations. The usage of Spanish among Mexican Americans is thought of as expressing (and expressive of) ethnic solidarity" (1976:336).

CHAPTER 2

Statement of the Problem

Persistence in retaining Spanish across generations is a characteristic of the U.S. Mexican community. The low profile of academic achievement among Mexicans has raised criticism that Spanish presents a barrier to Hispanic academic achievement. However, research has failed to fully explore the impact that Spanish has on the academic achievement of Mexicans.

The previous chapter demonstrated that Hispanic youths drop out from high school prior to completing their high school diploma at a rate of 45% annually (Trueba 1989). Research has also revealed that Hispanics drop out at higher rates even when background, economic and linguistic factors are controlled. Mexicans, who account for two-thirds of the U.S. Hispanic population, contribute nearly 75% of the Hispanic dropouts (United States Department of Education 1992c).

Hispanic communities, particularly Mexican communities, often display some of the factors associated with dropping out, such as low SES, a low parental educational level, and high rates of sibling dropouts (e.g. Ekstrom et al. 1987). In the school environment, Hispanic youth are known to display many of the characteristics associated with dropping out such as being overage, receiving low grades, and exhibiting high rates of truancy and disciplinary problems (e.g. Ekstrom et al. 1987). The high rate of retention of Spanish in Hispanic communities, motivated by a strong cultural connection to the language, has been suggested as interfering with academic achievement. Empirical research, however, is lacking in defining the impact that the use of and attitudes toward Spanish may have on academic achievement. Additionally, many of the sociolinguistic studies involving Mexican populations have focused on populations in the Southwest, ignoring the Mexican population residing in the Midwest.

Thus, because Hispanics, and Mexicans in particular, distinguish themselves from other linguistic minorities, further research is needed to explore their unique characteristics. Further, such research is particularly needed regarding the understudied Mexican population in the Midwest. The low academic achievement of Hispanics in the U.S. compels us to examine the impact that Spanish has across different academic levels. Therefore, the present study explores the role that the use of Spanish and the attitudes toward Spanish have in serving as indicators of academic achievement among Mexican youth in the Midwest.

2.1 FOCUS OF THE STUDY

The present study examines the patterns of usage of Spanish and English in daily interaction of bilingual youths of Mexican descent from an urban Midwest area (Chicago). The study also examines the attitudes expressed toward both Spanish and English by these individuals. Furthermore, this study examines the relationship of these sociolinguistic factors with academic achievement by comparing data from Mexican informants at three separate academic levels: High School Dropouts, High School Students and College Students.

2.2. RESEARCH QUESTIONS

The areas of interest in this study are the sociodemographic background, the academic background, and the sociolinguistic background of the informants and their relationship with academic level (High School Dropouts, High School Students or College Students). The questions guiding the investigation are the following:

1. Are current Hispanic high school students and/or college students similar to high school dropouts with respect to their sociodemographic profile?

The literature regarding dropouts has cited several sociodemographic factors as indicators of dropping out. Among the most prevalent are: low socioeconomic status, large family size, high rate of employment among students, low educational level of parents and siblings, immigrant status and belonging to a minority group. The present study seeks to examine the applicability of these factors in accurately identifying the academic achievement of Mexican-American students. If accurate, low achieving students should display a large number of these characteristics. High achieving students, on the other hand, should exhibit a minimum of these negative traits.

2. Are current Hispanic high school students and/or college students similar to high school dropouts with respect to their academic profile?

The academic traits that are frequently cited as harbingers of dropping out are low grade point average, one or more years of retention, enrollment in a non-academic curricular track, a high rate of truancy, one or more incidences of suspension or expulsion from school, a lack of participation in extracurricular activities, a lack of time spent on studying, a lack of parental support, low self-esteem and a low sense of having control over the outcomes one experiences. More controversial and less studied are the long-term effects that participation in bilingual education courses or in courses taught in the student's heritage language have on the academic achievement of students.

Similar to the preceding argument regarding the sociodemographic factors, the accuracy of the academic traits will be determined by their ability to distinguish students at different levels of academic achievement. That is, for these academic traits to be valid indicators of student academic outcomes, low achieving students should display a profile that contains a number of these negative indicators. In contrast, students who have been academically successful should exhibit relatively few of these traits.

3. Are current high school students and/or college students similar to high school dropouts with respect to their sociolinguistic profile regarding language use and language attitudes?

Given that language is popularly assumed to be one of the key factors in determining the academic success of language minority students, it is of utmost importance to explore the long-term effects that language has in affecting the academic outcomes of students. We are thus compelled to examine whether students at different levels of academic achievement differ with respect to the first language(s) in which they learned to speak, read and write and explore whether or not individuals at distinct academic levels differ with respect to their current profile of use of and attitudes toward Spanish and English.

If Spanish is truly a hindrance to the academic achievement of U.S. Mexican students, then those who have not succeeded academically will be expected to display a sociolinguistic profile that reveals early and persistent exposure to Spanish, will be expected to exhibit a high degree of Spanish proficiency, which purportedly would simultaneously serve to limit the student's English proficiency. Low achieving students would also be expected to use Spanish in a high number of their daily activities and exhibit attitudes which favor Spanish over English. By the same token, if the Spanish limits the educational outcomes of students then academically successful students would be expected to display a minimum of contact with the language. That is to say, that if language is detrimental to academic achievement, then successful students would be expected to have had limited exposure to Spanish, would be expected to possess a low level of proficiency in Spanish, counterbalanced with a high level of proficiency in English. It would then follow that with regard to attitudes, academically successful students would be expected to highly esteem English while holding Spanish is less high regard.

The following chapters present the methodology employed in investigating these questions, discuss the results from the demographic and academic data which confirm some, but not all, of the sociodemographic and academic attributes associated with Hispanic dropouts found in previous research. The results found regarding the patterns of language use and language attitudes across the three academic levels, provide evidence of the existence of linguistic ties to academic achievement. data. The final chapter presents a discussion of the overall findings.

CHAPTER 3

Methodology

The sample of informants who participated in this study consisted of Mexican youths living in the Midwest. The informants came from three different academic levels: High School Dropouts, High School Students and College Students.

Interviews were conducted with High School Dropout informants to explore whether the sociodemographic and academic characteristics they exhibited were consistent with those found for dropouts in the literature. The High School Dropout informants in this study represent the group that has had the least amount of success academically, thus, the data they provide serve as a basis for the investigation into the relationship between language and academic success.

Data from High School Student informants can be used to compare the sociodemographic, academic, and sociolinguistic characteristics exhibited by the High School Dropout informants were different from those of the general population of students that are attending high school in the Chicago area. Similarly, the College Student informants, representing individuals at the highest academic level, provide sociodemographic, academic and sociolinguistic characteristics regarding academically successful bilinguals.

Data were collected by means of a survey questionnaire presented in oral form to High School Dropout informants and in written form to High School Student and College Student informants. Additional data regarding language proficiency were collected from High School Student and College Student informants by means of a Spanish Vocabulary measure. The data collected from the three groups of informants provided the opportunity to explore the nature of the relationship between academic achievement and the use of and attitudes toward Spanish and English.

3.1 SAMPLE

The sample of High School Dropout informants interviewed for this study consisted of 38 individuals residing in the Chicago area who had dropped out from high school prior to completing the requirements for a degree.[1] All 38 informants were of Mexican descent, were living in the city of Chicago and had attended a Chicago public high school. Twenty-one of the informants were male; 17 of the informants were female. Thirty-four of those interviewed were between the ages of 16 and 30; only four male informants were over 30.[2]

Sixteen of the informants interviewed were contacted at Chicago-area educational centers offering General Educational Development (GED) classes. Interviews with these individuals were conducted during the first week of classes to limit the effects that a renewed exposure to an academic environment might have on their responses. The remaining 22 individuals were contacted through referrals from the informants themselves or from referrals made by acquaintances of the researchers.[3]

Data from High School Student informants provided a basis of comparison for High School Dropout informants to see whether the sociodemographic, academic, and sociolinguistic characteristics exhibited by the High School Dropout informants were different from those of the general population of students who are attending high school in the Chicago area. The sample of High School Student informants interviewed consisted of a total of 188 students attending Benito Juárez High School (BJHS), the Chicago Public High School with the most concentrated Latino population.[4] According to the school's 1994 School Report Card, 99.0% of the 1,995 BJHS students are Latino. The 188 informants were all of Mexican descent, ranging in age from 15 to 19 years old. One hundred eighteen (63%) of the High School Student informants were male and 70 (37%) were female.[5] Regarding class rank, one (.5%) was a freshman, 67 (35.6%) were sophomores, 52 (27.6%) were juniors and 68 (36.1%) were seniors.

All high school students are required by the State of Illinois to receive credit in a minimum of four English classes to graduate, thus informants were obtained from 13 English classes, 6 at the sophomore level (Basic English), 3 at the junior level (English Literature) and 4 at the senior level (World Literature and Creative Writing) in order to gain the greatest degree of access to the general student population. The particular English classes were selected by Mr. Jay Swanson, Vice-principal at BJHS, based on the researcher's request to interview at least 75 students from each class level and roughly equal numbers of students in both academic and non-academic tracks at each of the three class levels.

The sample of College Students consisted of a total of 36 students interviewed on the campus of the University of Illinois at Urbana-Champaign.[6] All 36 College Student informants were students of Mexican descent currently enrolled at the University of Illinois and ranged in age from 18 to 23. Thirteen (36.1%) of the College Student informants were male and 23 (63.9%) were female. Nine (25.0%) were freshmen, 6 (16.7%) were sophomores, 9 (25.0%) were juniors, 11 (30.6%) were seniors, and one (2.8%) was a first semester graduate student.

Informants were obtained by contacting various campus units, student organizations and instructors who were in frequent contact with Latino students. Flyers soliciting volunteers were also posted at prominent campus locations. Additionally, students were personally invited to participate by the researcher at various campus locations.

3.2 VARIABLES OF THE STUDY

Since the intent of the present study is to compare various background characteristics of students from different levels of academic success, and explore how these factors were related to the informant's current level of academic achievement, the study needed to document the factors that were inherent to the informant and his/her home environment, examine the factors that shaped the informant's educational experiences, and record the linguistic influences to which the informant had been and/or continued to be exposed. Thus, the variables in the study were divided into three separate areas: sociodemographic, academic and sociolinguistic.

The sociodemographic items explored the social background of the informants. The variables that were considered for analysis included the informant's age, sex, birthplace, age of arrival to the U.S. (if applicable), preferred term employed by the informant to express his/her ethnic identity, the occupations and educational levels of the informant's parents and the educational levels of the informant's siblings.

The academic variables, which were largely based on characteristics identified in the HS & B study (e.g. Ekstrom et al 1987), and modeled after statements used in Bachman Green and Wirtanen 1971, asked questions regarding achievement, the informant's participation in extracurricular activities, the informant's behavior in and out of school, and the support that was received at home. These items included grade point average (GPA), the curricular program (i.e. *"track"*) they pursued, the incidence of retention in school, the last grade informants had completed, their attendance and disciplinary records, their attitudes about school and self, the amount of academically-related parental support they received, the time they spent on academic vs. non-academic activities, and their record of employment while attending high school.[7]

The sociolinguistic variables in the study were designed to identify the amount of previous and current exposure the informant had had to Spanish and English in school and at home, record the informant's choice of either Spanish or English for different situations and/or for use with different conversational partners, and to explore the informants' attitudes toward both languages.

The sociolinguistic variables considered included factors of language use and language attitudes which are commonly examined (cf. Fishman, Cooper & Ma 1971, Weinreich 1974). These variables, which explored the informant's language proficiency and profiled the informant's language use. Sociolinguistic items included questions about the informant's first spoken, read and written language(s), a subjective evaluation of his/her current English and Spanish proficiencies.

Also included were variables recording information on the informant's regular conversational partners. The variables considered are similar to those found in previous research (e.g. Thompson 1974, Elías-Olivares 1976b, García et al 1988)and included the age difference between the informant and each interlocutor, the familial relationship, the interlocutor's place of birth, the informant's estimate of each interlocutor's level of proficiency in Spanish and English, the language(s) in which conversations were normally carried out with each interlocutor and the topic(s) of conversation normally discussed with each interlocutor.[8]

Other items, some modeled after Cooper and Fishman (1977), others inspired by the conclusions of Dornic (1978), were also included regarding the informant's choice of language when engaging in leisure activities (e.g. reading, thinking), when affected by emotional states (e.g. happy, mad), or when accomplishing a given purpose (e.g. arguing, explaining something mechanical).

A subgroup of variables related to language choice informants made in reference to the topics of conversation in which they were likely to engage with interlocutors.[9] Topics ranged from formal to informal in nature and were chosen based on the findings of previous research (e.g. Solé 1976, Carranza and Ryan 1975). The topic options included in the questionnaire were *politics, religion, school, medical issues, family issues, childhood or past, dreams and hopes, other* (an open category).

Another subgroup of language use variables was related to the appropriateness of a topic were adapted from Cooper and Fishman (1977). Informants responded to each item as either *Spanish, English* or *Both* depending on which language(s) they felt were most appropriate for use in discussing each of the following topics: *science, military commands, religious rituals, politics, novels, poetry, folksongs, bargaining, jokes, cursing, baby talk, lying,* and *persuading.*

Other sociolinguistic variables included a set of language attitude statements which reflected *affective, integrative* and *instrumental* attitudes as well as feelings of *language loyalty.* Statements for these items were based on previous research (e.g. Cooper and Fishman 1974, 1977; Attinasi 1979, 1985; Hakuta and D'Andrea 1992). Informants' responses to language attitude items were recorded as *agree, disagree* or *undecided.*

Likewise, a measure was presented in order to further assess an informant's affinity toward Spanish.[10] The *semantic differential,* a measure developed by Osgood (1964) and widely used in language attitude studies (cf. Galván et al. 1976, Cooper and Fishman 1977), recorded responses about Spanish on a five-point Likert scale ranging between two semantically opposed adjectives. The positive adjectives with their accompanying negative counterparts in parentheses are: *beautiful (ugly), rich (poor), musical (noisy), precise (vague), logical (illogical), sophisticated (simple), rhythmical (irregular), refined (vulgar), colorful (bland), public (private), superior (inferior), pure (impure), soothing (unnerving), graceful (clumsy),* and *sacred (profane).*

3.3 INSTRUMENT

Data from the three samples of informants was collected by using two instruments. The first, a survey questionnaire, was administered orally to the High School Dropout informants and presented in written form to the High School Student and College Student informants. Additional data regarding language proficiency was collected by means of a Spanish vocabulary measure. This measure was only administered to High School Student and College Student informants.[11]

3.3.1 Questionnaire

The instrument used to elicit the data for the High School Dropout informants consisted of a package which contained a letter of introduction, an answer guide that provided responses to multiple choice items, and an interview questionnaire. This information was constructed in both English and Spanish to allow for the informants' preferences of language for the interview.[12] The High School Dropout questionnaire consisted of 35 sections of items, several of which contained a number of subparts that either elaborated a theme or elicited specific detail about a given item. Most answers could be selected from a set of responses provided on the accompanying answer guide.

Ten sections containing a total of 23 items were devoted to soliciting sociodemographic information as described previously. An additional 16 sections containing 46 items were used to record information pertaining to the informant's academic background, particularly those characteristics which the literature often identified with students who dropped out from high school. The remaining nine sections were designed to elicit information related to the informants' language choice (six sections, 51 items) and language attitudes (three sections, 53 items).

Information about the attitudes informants have toward Spanish and English was assessed by means of responses of *agree, disagree or undecided* to statements reflecting *language loyalty, affective, instrumental* and *integrative* attitudes. Statements were modeled after previous research and were asked separately about English and Spanish. In general, the statements in each section were constructed in a parallel manner such that the same statements were asked in both sections, differing only in the language to which they referred in each section.[13] Other language attitude measures included a *Language*

Appropriateness Index and a *Semantic Differential Scale* described above.

The questionnaire used to collect data for the High School Student informants was a modified version of the questionnaire used to interview the High School Dropout informants. Some questions on the High School Dropout questionnaire that had generated a number of requests for clarification from the informants were eliminated due to a lack of clarity. Other questions were eliminated since they had been included in the High School Dropout survey as part of another project involving the influence friends have on dropping out. Still other questions were eliminated since they specifically explored the circumstances surrounding the informant's decision to drop out from high school and thus lacked applicability to the High School Student population. Questions that were not on the High School Dropout questionnaire that were added to the High School Student questionnaire included questions regarding the current grade level of students, their highest academic goal and their future intended occupation.

Questions retained their multiple-choice or fill-in-the-blank format from the High School Dropout questionnaire, however, the options for all but two questions that required responses in a multiple choice format were provided within the questionnaire rather than as a separate answer guide to reduce confusion in responding. An answer guide was still retained, however, for two items and was provided on the reverse of the first page that contained a letter of introduction similar to the letter provided to the High School Dropout informants. Other questions were modified to clarify language choice options.[14] Items on the High School Dropout questionnaire that had referred to past high school experiences were changed to the present tense. All items were renumbered as necessary.

The resulting questionnaire was provided in English and in Spanish to allow for the informants' preferences of language for the questionnaire.[15] The High School Student questionnaire consisted of 27 sections of items, several of which, as in the High School Dropout questionnaire, contained a number of subparts that elaborated a theme or solicited specific detail about a given item.

As in the High School Dropout questionnaire, items in the High School Student questionnaire elicited information regarding an informant's sociodemographic background, his/her academic background, his/her patterns of use of Spanish and English, and his/her attitudes toward Spanish and English. Twelve sections containing a total of 20 items were devoted to eliciting sociodemographic information, six sections containing 19 items were used to record information pertaining to the informant's academic background. The remaining 10 sections were devoted to assessing the informants' use and attitudes toward Spanish and English. Seven of the sections totaling 101 items addressed the informants' use of Spanish and English and three sections totaling 53 items explored the informants' attitudes toward Spanish and English.

The questionnaire used to collect data from the College Student informants was adapted from the High School Student version of the survey instrument. No items were eliminated from the High School Student version in constructing the College Student version, however three items were added to record the informant's university GPA, the informant's field of concentration (major), and to identify the high school the informant had attended. Other items were modified contextually in order to be better adapted to the College Student population.

The resulting College Student questionnaire contained 12 sections of 20 items regarding sociodemographic information, and six sections of 22 items regarding academic background. The 10 sections remaining in the questionnaire explored the sociolinguistic characteristics of the informants including seven sections of 101 items that concerned language choice and three sections of 53 items that explored language attitudes. Versions of the College Student questionnaire were prepared in both English and Spanish and were made equally available to the College Student informants.

A full description of the modifications made to the original High School Dropout questionnaire to form the High School Student questionnaire, as well as the modifications to the High School Student questionnaire to develop the College Student questionnaire can be found in the Appendix.

3.3.2 Spanish vocabulary list

Self-reported language skills have been criticized for lack of accuracy and for the potential of influence by attitudinal factors (Hakuta & D'Andrea 1992). However, Bachman & Palmer found that self-reported proficiencies "can be reliable and valid measures of communicative language abilities" (1989:22).

In order to provide a more quantifiable, objective measure to verify the informants' subjective assessment of their proficiency in Spanish, a separate measure of language proficiency was added to the High School Student and College Student questionnaires. Popular standardized measures (e.g. Test of Adult Basic Education (TABE) 1994) were rejected due to their heavy emphasis on literacy skills and their lack of sensitivity to dialectal variation which bias them against populations that lack exposure to formal Spanish or whose oral abilities may exceed their reading abilities.

Research in first and second language reading has provided evidence of a strong correlation between vocabulary knowledge and reading ability (see Hancin-Bhatt & Nagy, 1994 for a review of the literature). Based on these results, it was proposed that vocabulary knowledge could also be related to one's ability to comprehend and speak in a language, Thus, a measure assessing vocabulary knowledge would provide reliable insight into the informants' overall language proficiency.

The vocabulary measure selected for use in the present study was adapted from one of the measures used by Hancin-Bhatt & Nagy (1994) to explore the transfer of knowledge from cognates of 4th, 6th and 8th grade Spanish-English bilingual students. Informants in that study indicated whether or not they knew the meaning of a Spanish word by circling either "Sí" or "No"; distractors were included in the measure to keep the students from guessing randomly. This measure was adapted for use with mature learners by having the informants select the appropriate English translations of the Spanish words on the measure. Additionally, a bias toward literacy was eliminated by providing a simultaneous presentation of the words, clearly pronounced, on tape.

In order to select the words for the vocabulary measure, a pilot list of 105 words, representing fifteen words for each of seven semantic categories found on the questionnaire *(politics, religion, school, medical issues, family issues, childhood, dreams)* was selected based on the researcher's past interactions with native Spanish speakers in the Chicago area. Furthermore, since Hancin-Bhatt & Nagy (1994) found evidence of bilinguals, particularly mature bilinguals, successfully transferring the knowledge of orthographically similar words from one language to another, all words were non-cognates.

The list of 105 words was submitted to 15 speakers of Spanish (12 Native, 3 near-Native) residing in the Chicago area for evaluation. Individuals were asked to provide their opinion, on a four-point Likert scale, of how frequently each word was heard or used in daily conversation (see Frequency Judgement Test in the Appendix).

Words that were ranked very common were scored as four, words that were somewhat common were scored as three, and so on in order to calculate the average frequency for each word. Words for each semantic category were divided into three levels according to the average of their rated frequencies. Words whose frequency averaged below two were considered low frequency. Words whose average frequency ranged above two and below three were considered medium frequency. Finally, words whose average frequency was three or above were considered high frequency.

For each of the seven semantic categories, six words were selected, consisting of two words from each frequency level. When possible, the two words selected from each frequency level consisted of one noun and one verb. In two instances where there weren't enough words in the low frequency level, the lowest medium frequency word was selected (i.e. *acatar, huésped*) (see Appendix). The resulting 42 words were listed in alphabetical order and randomly interspersed with eight Spanish-like nonsense words.

Next to each of the 50 words were four columns. The first three columns contained, in random order, the true English translation of the Spanish word (e.g. *alcalde*, "mayor"; *éxito*, "success") and two false English translations of the Spanish word. One of the false translations represented a word from the same semantic category as the Spanish word (e.g. *alcalde*, "senator"; *éxito*, "dream"). The other false translation provided was a cognate that either resembled the translation of a phonologically similar Spanish word (e.g. *alcalde*, "soup" [*caldo*]) or resembled an orthographically similar English word (e.g. *éxito*, "exit"). The fourth column was labeled simply "Not a word". The measure is provided in its entirety in the Appendix.

An audiotape of the 50 words (42 test items and 8 nonsense words) were recorded by a native speaker of Spanish. Each word was pronounced twice clearly and at a deliberate pace so as to allow participants sufficient time to mark their answers. The tape lasted 6.5 minutes.

3.4 DATA COLLECTION

Data for High School Dropout informants was collected during the Summer of 1993 by means of oral interviews conducted by three bilingual researchers. All of the interviews were conducted in person with the exception of three that were conducted over the telephone with individuals who were unable to schedule a personal session.

At the beginning of each session, the interviewer asked the informant which language they preferred to proceed with the interview. Once the selection of language was made, a brief letter of consent was presented for the informant to read. The letter provided a general outline of the study being undertaken, assured the informant's anonymity, and thanked them for their willingness to participate. The interviewer orally summarized the contents of the letter to ensure that the informant was aware of its contents and presented the informant with a copy of the full questionnaire for inspection and an *answer guide* that would be used throughout the interview.[16] The interviewer also told the informants of their right to refuse to answer any questions that they felt were too personal or offensive.[17]

During each interview, the interviewer read each question to the informant and recorded each response on a *code sheet* (see Appendix).[18] If at any time the informant was unsure of the question being asked, the interviewer provided a brief explanation of the question and reminded the informant that there were no right or wrong answers. Unnecessary sections were skipped if the informant's previous response indicated that further exploration of a given item was unwarranted. In all, the questionnaire took an average of 30 minutes to complete. After each interview was concluded, the interviewer thanked the informant for his or her assistance in the study and asked the informant for referrals of other possible interviewees.

Data from High School Student informants was collected in the Spring semester of 1995 by the researcher accompanied by one bilingual assistant. Written survey questionnaires were completed individually as an in-class assignment during regular class periods.

At the beginning of each class period the researcher introduced herself and her assistant to the students and explained that their help was sought in filling out a questionnaire about language. Students were informed that the questionnaires were to be answered anonymously and were assured that their responses would not have any effect upon their grades, nor would individual responses be reviewed by any school officials. Students were also informed of their right to refuse to answer any question that they felt was too personal or offensive.[19] Questionnaires were then distributed to the students according to the language in which they requested to complete it. Pencils were also provided for filling out the survey.

Since students in high school English classes must demonstrate a reading level that is on par with that of their grade peers, the researcher did not feel it would be necessary to read each question as had been done for the High School Dropout informants. Thus, the researcher and assistant provided only general instructions regarding the completion of the survey and allowed the students to complete the questions at their own pace. As only seven of the students asked to complete the survey in Spanish, instructions for completing the survey were provided in English by the researcher to the class in general and were simultaneously translated into Spanish by the assistant to the 1-3 students in any given class period who asked to complete the questionnaire in Spanish.

The vocabulary measure was completed first. Informants were instructed that a tape would be played that pronounced all of the Spanish words in the leftmost column on the page and that their task was to circle what they considered to be the best English translation of the Spanish word from the words in the columns to the right. Informants were told that they were not expected to know all of the Spanish words and were further warned that not all of the Spanish words were real words, rather some Spanish words had been made up to keep them from guessing. Informants were told that if they had never heard one of the words on the list or if they did not know the word's meaning, they were to circle the phrase "Not a word".

To ensure that the students knew the definitions of all of the English words, the researcher asked students to review the entire list of English translations and invited them to ask for the (English) definition of any word which they did not know. When the researcher was satisfied that the students knew the definitions of all of the English words, she quickly reviewed the instructions on how to mark the answers and began the tape. The tape also reviewed the instructions on how to mark answers in both English and in Spanish prior to starting the pronunciation of the words.

Once the tape for the vocabulary measure was finished, the researcher instructed the students to mark their answers to the remaining items in the High School Student questionnaire by either filling in a blank, circling a choice, or placing a mark beside or below an option provided on the questionnaire. Detailed instructions were provided for item number 11, where students were asked to provide background information only about the people with whom they spoke on a regular basis. Students were instructed to fill in the age and sex of each interlocutor, the interlocutor's country of origin, the language the interlocutor spoke, the language the student used to speak to the interlocutor, and topic(s) of their conversation with each interlocutor.

For responses to sections in item 11 regarding the interlocutor's language proficiency, the informant's language choice when speaking to each interlocutor, and the topics of conversation with each interlocutor, students were told to refer to sections A and B of the Answer Guide which was printed on the reverse of the first page of the questionnaire. Students were shown how to fold up the cover sheet to reveal the answer guide.

Section A of the answer guide provided five language choice options ranging from Spanish only to English only. Students were told provide a number from one to five for their responses for both the language(s) they felt each interlocutor spoke, and the language(s) they chose to speak to each interlocutor and were told to provide the number in Section A that corresponded to their response for each item and for each interlocutor.

Responses for the section in item 11 regarding the topics of conversation with each interlocutor were made by circling any or all of the eight initials that represented possible topics of conversation. Informants were instructed to refer to section B of the answer guide.

Once these general instructions were completed, students were allowed to answer questions at their own pace with the researcher occasionally reminding them of how much time was left to fill out the questionnaire. The researcher and the assistant circulated among the students to provide assistance in filling out the questionnaire as needed. Individual assistance was provided to the students by both researcher and assistant in the language in which the student was completing the survey and/or the language in which the student requested assistance.

All High School Student Questionnaires were completed within a class time period which ranged from 45-55 minutes. All questionnaires were collected as they were finished. At the end of the period after all questionnaires had been completed, students were thanked for their participation and were allowed to keep the pencil (with the University of Illinois inscription) they had used to fill out the survey as a token of appreciation for their participation.

Data from College Student informants were collected during the Spring semester of 1995. College Student informants completed questionnaires on a volunteer walk-in basis during survey sessions announced by the researcher or during an appointment mutually agreed upon by the researcher and informant. All students who demonstrated an interest in answering the questionnaire were allowed to do so and all students who completed the questionnaire received a small token of appreciation from the researcher. All interviews took place in a formal setting: either the researcher's office, a departmental conference room or a classroom.

Administration of the College Student questionnaires was similar to that of the High School Student questionnaires. College Student informants were asked the language in which they preferred to complete the questionnaire and were orally informed of the general purpose of the study, assured of their anonymity and their right to decline to answer any questions s/he felt were objectionable. Informants were then presented with a letter of introduction that provided this information in writing. Informants were then asked to first complete the Spanish vocabulary measure and were provided with the same instructions as had the High School Student informants. Once the tape for the vocabulary measure had finished, College Student informants were provided with the same general instructions for completing the survey that the High School Student informants had received. College Student informants were then allowed to complete the survey at their own pace.[20] College Student informants took no more than 30 minutes to complete the survey.

3.5 STATISTICAL ANALYSIS

Initial statistical analyses were performed on an IBM version of SPSS; supplemental analyses were prepared using Mystat for the Macintosh and Microsoft Excel. As the majority of the data was categorical in nature, most of the analyses consisted of frequency summaries. Where a possible relationship between two variables was suspected, chi-squared cross tabulations or Pearson product-moment correlations were computed to confirm or disconfirm the association. The results of the analyses are presented in the following chapter.

NOTES

1. Three individuals from a total sample of 41 High School Dropout informants did not meet the background requirements since they were Puerto Rican. Their responses were eliminated from the analysis.

2. These four males were aged 31, 35, 38 and 46, respectively.

3. These 22 informants, who were not contacted at a GED learning center, were not specifically questioned regarding whether or not they had considered returning to school to obtain a GED.

4. Four informants from the total sample of 192 individuals were eliminated from the analysis for not being of Mexican descent.

5. The reason for the unequal numbers of males and females is unknown.

6. The original College Student sample consisted of a pool of 64 individuals, however, 28 informants did not meet background requirements, thus their responses were eliminated from the analysis. Of those eliminated, 11 were non-Latino, 16 were Latino but were not of Mexican origin, and one was a high school student who was on campus visiting her sister.

7. Some sociodemographic and academic items were eliminated from consideration prior to the analysis. Some of the eliminated items had been specifically added to the questionnaire to explore the impact of friendship on academic achievement for a Summer research project conducted by a research assistant (items 8, 9, 10, 24a-i), others were later found to be vague or misleading (items 17, 22e, 23a, 23d, 26c-e, 27 [except for number of hours worked], 31a-e) (see Appendix).

8. In this item space was provided for multiple interlocutors of the same category (e.g. siblings). Additionally, for the ease of the interview process, a list of eight topics (*politics, religion, school, medical issues, family issues, dreams, childhood/past* and *other*) was provided. Only the *other* category was open-ended.

9. Informants were allowed to choose as many topics as they liked, of the ones provided, for each interlocutor, and if none of the topics were relevant to what was normally discussed with a given interlocutor, the informant was given the opportunity to provide free responses in the *other* category.

10. Since we were more interested in exploring the informants' attitudes toward Spanish, this measure was not done for English.

11. This measure was developed after the interviews of the High School Dropout informants had been completed. Due to the anonymity of all informants, it was not possible to later return to the High School Dropout informants to administer this additional measure.

12. Of a total of 38 interviews, 33 of the interviews were conducted in English; five were conducted in Spanish.

13. The Spanish section included two additional statements that were not part of the English section: "Bilingual Education should help everyone develop Spanish skills." and "When you have children you want them to learn Spanish." The English counterparts to these statements were deemed illogical for the

context of the U.S. and not included. Additionally, to elicit a more clear contrast between the two languages, the question "Spanish is an important part of Latino culture." was paired with "English is a threat to Latino culture."

14. The option "Mixed Spanish and English" was added to provide an option for code-switching (see Appendix).

15. Of the 188 surveys completed, seven were in Spanish and 181 were in English.

16. The *answer guide* allowed the researchers to save space on the questionnaire by providing a summary of answers that were to be used several times during the interview.

17. There were no refusals to answer any of the questions.

18. The *codesheet* was a simplified version of the questionnaire used only by the researchers for the purpose of more efficiently recording the answers given by the informants (see Appendix).

19. High School Student informants occasionally skipped items, but this was generally attributed to the informant's confusion or carelessness. Only two informants on two separate items refused to provide information.

20. Similar to High School Student informants, some College Student informants skipped some items. This again was attributed to oversight since no College Student informants communicated any offense or reservation about answering any of the items.

CHAPTER 4

Variables Related to Academic Achievement

The present study examined the sociodemographic, academic and sociolinguistic characteristics of Midwestern youths of Mexican descent at three separate academic levels. Several of the sociodemographic and academic factors that were outlined in the literature and examined here distinguished themselves as strong indicators of academic achievement among Midwest Mexican youths bilingual in English and Spanish. Others of these variables, while important indicators of academic achievement for the general population, were shown to be indicators of only moderate strength for the samples here. These results are outlined in sections 4.1 and 4.2 below.

The sociolinguistic profile of the High School Dropout, High School Student and College Student informants is presented in section 4.3. These analyses revealed that Spanish, either solely or in combination with English, was more often the first language to which informants all groups were exposed which corroborated Solé's (1990) claim that more than 50% of school aged Hispanics are incipient bilinguals in English. Other results revealed that informants overall felt more confident regarding their English skills than their Spanish skills. Nonetheless, informants at higher academic levels were more likely than informants at lower levels to rate their Spanish skills highly and were seen to employ Spanish to a greater extent in their personal language choices. Language use for interpersonal conversations was seen to have similar patterns across all academic levels. The patterns were seen to be primarily regulated by the language proficiency of the interlocutor, the place of birth of the interlocutor, and the age difference between the interlocutor and the informant. Topic of conversation was seen to play a minor role in the choice of language. Topics in general, however, were shown to be more often associated with "Either" or "Both" Spanish and English rather than with either language alone, although some tendencies toward one language or the other were also noted.

Regarding language attitudes it was found that all groups displayed positive attitudes toward Spanish. Moreover, on several variables a regular increase in frequency of informants declaring positive *affective, instrumental, integrative* and *language loyalty* attitudes toward Spanish was noted as academic level rose. Such a pattern suggests that certain positive attitudes are associated with academic achievement.

It was also found that studying a Midwestern Mexican population provided valuable information regarding populations outside of the Southwest. Contrary to what is characteristic of southwestern Mexican populations, informants in this study were shown to attribute an instrumental value to Spanish as well as to English. Moreover, on several of the attitude measures, informants of all groups were shown to attribute positive feelings toward both Spanish and English to a comparable degree. Additionally, rises in positive attitudes toward Spanish that were seen across academic level on some variables were, at times, accompanied decreases in attitudes toward English.

Informants were also found to contrast in terms of their language use, but not attitudes, with other Midwest informants. While Attinasi (1985) found that Spanish was used to such a low degree as to prevent its perpetuation, only the High School Dropout informants displayed an overall low use of Spanish. High School Student and College Student informants employed Spanish in both interpersonal and personal contexts. The positive attitudes expressed by informants in this study toward favoring the maintenance of Spanish and wanting children to speak Spanish were found to be similar to Attinasi's results.

4.1 SOCIODEMOGRAPHIC PROFILE

Regarding native background, informants for the present study were found to differ from informants for previous research on Hispanic dropouts. While Valverde's (1986) findings for Texas Hispanics indicated that high school graduates were more likely to be foreign born, the present study found that individuals at higher academic levels were more likely to be U.S. born (High School Student 73.4%; College Student 72.2%) than were dropouts (55.3%). The reason behind this difference between Midwestern and Southwestern Mexican populations may lie in the overall recency of immigration of the Midwesterners. Solé (1990: Table 6) reports that less than 20% of Mexicans in most Southwest states is foreign born as opposed to 44.4% in Illinois. In the present study less than half of the informants from each group was reported to have been born abroad, however, 65.8% of the High School Dropout informants, 80.9% of the High School Student informants, and 83.3% of the College Student informants, had at least one parent that had been born abroad. Thus the informants in all three groups, if not immigrants themselves, were very likely to be first generation Americans.

Regardless of their country of origin, but perhaps in accordance with their recent immigration status, informants in all three groups displayed a high degree of cultural loyalty to Mexico, evident in the informants' preference for the term "Mexican" to identify themselves culturally over other terms (see Table 1). In all groups, a preference was noted for a global term, either "Hispanic" (preferred second to "Mexican" by High School Dropout and High School Student informants) or "Latino" (preferred second to "Mexican" by College Student informants) for cultural identity.[1] Noted also was the fact that this preference for a global term increased with academic attainment, suggesting that more educated informants feel a greater connection with a wider Spanish-speaking community, perhaps as a result of the broader cultural experiences that accompany higher levels of education. This result corroborates Hurtado and Gurín's (1987) findings of a connection between a global, pan-Hispanic term and social mobility.

This strong cultural tie noted for all informants does not, however, hinder students academically as can be seen when the figures for the two most popular terms are taken as a whole: "Mexican" or "Hispanic" is preferred by 89.5% of High School Dropout informants, while "Mexican" or "Latino" is preferred by 88.9% of College Student informants. Thus, informants at both academic extremes exhibit strong ethnic identity in roughly equal proportion.

Several items revealed that the socioeconomic background of the informants from all three groups was similar. High School Dropout, High School Student, and College Student informant groups as a whole reported an average number of *siblings* (4.316, 3.867, 4.000,

Table 1. Three most common ethnic terms identified by informants.

	High School Dropouts %	High School Students %	College Students %
Mexican	76.3	52.7	66.7
Hispanic/Latino	13.2	19.2	22.2
Mexican-American	5.3	6.4	5.6

respectively) higher than the average number of total offspring for a household for a general population (2.58), but also exceeded the same figure for U.S. Hispanics (3.84) (Wright 1993: 282). This means that large family size, since it is prevalent across all three academic levels, is not a useful indicator of academic achievement among Midwest Mexicans.

Parental occupations may exert a moderate influence over academic achievement, however, the influence may be more tied to the father's occupation than to the mother's (see Table 2). Families in all three groups derived income from low skilled positions, however, the overall rate of labor participation (i.e. the proportion of persons known to be employed outside of the home) was seen to decrease for mothers and increase for fathers as academic level of the informants rose. Moreover, a rise in academic achievement accompanied an increased rate of employment in mid-skilled and high skilled and professional positions on the part of the fathers. A similar trend was not noted, however, for the mothers of the informants. Given the unequal salary structure discussed in Chapter 1, it is reasonable to assume that an increase in both rate and level of employment on the part of the fathers provides a stabilizing effect on the family's economic status, which in turn may be conducive to higher levels of academic achievement.

Related to the economic stability of the family is the number of parents in the home. While noted that this trait was not directly assessed, the educational and occupational information provided by the informants about their parents was used as a rough guide. Such information was most consistently supplied by College Student informants suggesting that informants at the highest level of academic achievement maintained closer ties with both parents than did either High School Dropout or High School Student informants. Nonetheless, this variable appears less important, and is perhaps subsumed by the overall occupational information of the family.

Table 2. Parents' occupations.

	Mothers			Fathers		
	High School Dropouts	High School Students	College Students	High School Dropouts	High School Students	College Students
	%	%	%	%	%	%
Unknown status	0.0	25.5	0.0	21.1	25.5	13.8
Not employed outside the home	39.5	31.4	55.6	18.4	4.8	0.0
Low skilled (Laborer)	44.7	36.7	33.3	57.9	52.1	55.6
Mid-skilled (Supervisor)	5.3	1.6	2.8	0.0	10.6	13.9
High-skilled (Manager)	2.6	3.7	8.3	0.0	2.7	11.1
Professional (Owner)	7.9	1.1	0.0	2.6	4.3	5.6
	100.0	100.0	100.0	100.0	100.0	100.0

The occupational status of the informants themselves while in high school was not able to be assessed with regard to its relationship to academic achievement due to lack of information. Too few of the High School Dropout and High School Student informants in this study were employed while in high school to allow an examination of the influence of this trait. Also, data were lacking on College Student informants to provide a comparison.

The low occupational level of the parents of the informants mirrors their low level of education (see Table 3)[2]. For all three groups no more than 45% of either the mothers or the fathers of the informants were reported as having minimally a high school degree. Nevertheless, while the overall profile of the parents' education is low, the data do suggest that there may be a link to academic achievement associated with parental educational level which is biased toward the fathers. Parents of College Student informants were nearly twice as likely than parents of either High School Dropout or High School Student informants to hold high school diplomas suggesting that children of parents who hold a high school diploma are more likely to attend college. Fathers also demonstrated small, yet noticeable increases in level of education as the academic level of the informants rose.

Table 3. Parents' educational level.*

	Mothers			Fathers		
	High School Dropouts	High School Students	College Students	High School Dropouts	High School Students	College Students
	%	%	%	%	%	%
Less than HS Graduate	65.8	51.1	55.6	60.5	44.6	47.2
HS Graduate	15.8	14.4	33.3**	15.8	12.2	27.8***
Some College/Trade School	5.3	3.2	8.3	0.0	2.1	5.6***
College/Trade School Graduate	2.6	2.1	2.8	2.6	3.2	11.1***
Total	89.5	70.8	100.0	78.9	62.1	91.7

*Columns that do not add to 100% indicate that educational information was lacking.

**Mothers: (2, $N = 63.5$) = 10.479, p≤.01;

***Fathers: HS Graduate (2, $N = 55.8$) = 7.174, p≤.05; Some College (2, $N = 7.7$) = 6.236, p≤.05; College Graduate (2, $N = 16.9$) = 7.989, p≤.05

A more clear indicator of academic achievement, however, was provided by the educational profile of the siblings of the informants. Siblings exhibited a greatly improved educational profile over that of their parents, however, differences were noted between groups (see Table 4). All three groups had similar proportions of siblings that had graduated from high school, suggesting that having siblings that had achieved a high school diploma was not influential in one's own attainment. Differences were found, however, in the number of siblings with college experience. While slightly over 40% of High School Dropout and High School Student informants reported having siblings that had attended a post-secondary institution, this contrasted sharply with the 80.6% of College Student informants who reported having siblings with college experience.

Table 4. Siblings' educational level.*

	High School Dropouts %	High School Students %	College Students %
College experience	47.4	41.5	80.6**
High School Graduate	44.7	36.7	38.9
High School Dropout	44.7	12.2	8.3**

*Although siblings are not duplicated between categories, informants could respond to more than one category according to the status of their various siblings.

**College: $(2, N = 169.5) = 15.727$, $p \leq .01$; HS Dropout: $(2, N = 65.2) = 36.754$, $p \leq .01$

Stark differences were also found in the proportion of siblings that had dropped out from high school. Some 44.7% of High School Dropout informants reported having siblings that had dropped out from high school; a figure nearly equal to both the proportion of siblings that had graduated high school, and the proportion of siblings that attended college for that group. At the High School Student level, however, only 12.2% of the reported having siblings that had not completed high school. This figure was further reduced for the College Student informants, only 8.3% of whom reported having siblings that had dropped out.

The data regarding sibling education confirm previous research (e.g. Ekstrom et al 1987) that individuals are more likely to drop out of high school when they have siblings who have done so before them. What has also been seen in this data however, is that an individual's likelihood of attending college is increased when they have siblings that have also attended college.

In sum, the most salient sociodemographic indicator of academic achievement of Mexicans in the Midwest appears to be sibling education. Parental occupational status and educational level also appear to influence academic achievement, but to a much more moderate degree. Factors such as family size and ethnic identity were not found to have any bearing on academic achievement.

4.2 ACADEMIC PROFILE

Informants were similar in the country in which they were educated: over 90% of the High School Dropout, High School Student and College Student informants experienced all of their formal education in the U.S., and primarily in the Chicago area. Nonetheless, informants from each group displayed a very different educational profile.

One of the first areas in which informants differed was in their exposure to bilingual education or Spanish-only education programs. As seen in Table 5, fewer than 25% of High School Dropout informants participated in programs where they were exposed to any Spanish in the classroom, either solely or in combination with English. In contrast, twice as many High School Student informants as High School Dropout informants reported having participated in bilingual or Spanish-only programs. College Student informants had the highest rate of participation in either type of program with over 50% having participated in bilingual programs and nearly 45% participating in Spanish Only programs. Thus, the degree of exposure to programs in which Spanish was used in the classroom increased dramatically with the academic level of the informants.

While the nature of the effect that exposure to Spanish in the classroom has not been explored in this study, the results suggest a net benefit derived from exposure to native language instruction. This finding counters public school policies that have traditionally encouraged little or no instruction to be provided in the language minority student's native tongue (cf. Durán 1983, Trueba 1989).

The three groups also differed with respect to the incidence of grade retention. As the academic level of the informants increased, a decrease was seen in the rate of students being held back (see Table 6). Moreover, not only did the incidence of retention decrease considerably across academic level, but the duration of the retention for those that had been held back diminished as well. That is to say, that High School Dropout informants were more likely to report having been held back in school and were more likely to have been retained for longer periods (up to four years) than the High School Student informants (up to two years). Likewise, College Student informants were the least likely of all to have been held back in school, and those who were held back were only retained for the period of a year.

Table 5. Informants reporting exposure to bilingual education or Spanish only education programs.*

	High School Dropouts %	High School Students %	College Students %
Bilingual Education	23.7	50.5	52.8**
Spanish Only Education	13.2	23.9	44.4**

*Informants could respond to both categories according to their educational experiences.

**Bilingual: $(2, N = 127) = 12.364$, $p \leq .01$; Spanish Only $(2, N = 81.5) = 18.505$, $p \leq .01$

Table 6. Informants retained in school.

	High School Dropouts %	High School Students %	College Students %	N	Chi-squared
Not retained	39.5	67.6	91.7	198.8	20.599*
Retained 1 year	44.7	30.9	8.3	83.9	24.149*
Retained 2 years	7.9	1.6	0.0	9.5	11.016*
Retained 3-4 years	5.3	0.0	0.0	5.3	10.600*

*For all, df= 2, $p \leq .01$

These results support those of earlier studies (e.g. Ekstrom et al 1987) which noted that dropouts were more likely to have been held back. Furthermore, given the high rate of retention experienced by the High School Dropout informants, these results indicate that being held back in school is related to the lack of overall academic attainment of Hispanic youths.

Dramatic differences between informant groups were again noted in the grades that informants of different academic levels reported receiving while in high school (see Table 7). High School Dropout informants were more likely to have reported receiving below average grades while in high school than either High School Student or College Student informants. High School Student informants reported receiving grades across the scale, however overall, the grades they received were more likely to be above average than not. College Student informants, on the other hand, unanimously reported receiving above average grades while attending high school.

The grades one receives during high school seem to be associated with academic achievement (e.g. Valdivieso 1986, Ekstrom et al 1987). These data may indicate then, that the 28.2% of the High School Student that reported receiving below average grades are at risk of dropping out.

Not all academic variables displayed such marked contrast across informant groups as do those in Tables 6 and 7. Although High School Dropout informants eventually dropped out, they reported having pursued an academic, general or vocational education while in high school at the same rate as the High School Student informants (see Table 8). College Student informants, on the other hand, were nearly five times as likely as either the High School Dropout or High School Student informants to have studied in an academic track. However, the fact that a large number of students of all levels studied in a general track demonstrates that the general track distinction is not a useful indicator of school leaving among the informants in this population.

The fact that the majority of College Student informants attended private high schools or public high schools that were more racially integrated corroborates the findings of Kyle et al. (1986) and suggests that these schools offered Latino students more educational opportunities. Alternately, data from the High School Student informants may be evidence that Latino high schools show a reluctance to placing large numbers of students in an academic track. Even so, a large number of College Student informants reported having been enrolled in a general education track during high school, suggesting that Latino students can advance academically in spite of being placed in a less challenging track.

Differences between informants from different academic levels were also noted with respect to behaviors that signaled disciplinary problems. As Table 9 demonstrates, High School Dropout informants were almost twice as likely as College Student informants to report having cut class, and were more than four times as likely as College Student informants to have been suspended from school. Surprisingly though, High School Student informants, rather than College Student informants were the least likely to have experienced problems in these areas.

Table 7. Informants' Grade Point Averages in high school.

	High School Dropouts %	High School Students %	College Students %	N	Chi-squared
A's	0	1.1	5.6	6.7	7.883*
A's and B's	13.2	13.8	58.31	85.3	47.065**
B's	0	6.9	25.0	31.9	31.355**
B's and C's	18.4	39.4	11.1	154.2	18.798**
C's	21.1	9.0	0	30.1	22.346**
C's and D's	23.7	24.5	0	48.2	24.120**
D's	7.9	.5	0	8.4	13.979**
D's and F's	13.2	3.2	0	16.4	17.346**
F's	2.6	0	0	2.6	5.2 ns

$*p \leq .05$, $**p \leq .01$, For all, df=2

Table 8. Percentage of informants enrolled in Academic, General and Vocational curriculums while attending high school.

	High School Dropouts %	High School Students %	College Students %	N	Chi-squared
Academic	10.5	10.1	50.0	70.6	44.651*
General	65.8	62.8	41.7	170.3	6.077**
Vocational	23.7	21.8	8.3	53.8	7.862**

$*df = 2$, $p \leq .01$ $**df = 2$, $p \leq .05$

Table 9. Percentage of informants reporting disciplinary problems while attending high school.*

	High School Dropouts %	High School Students %	College Students %	N	Chi-squared
Cut Class	89.5	37.2	50.0	176.7	25.237**
Suspended	76.3	2.5	16.7	95.5	96.337**

*Informants could respond to both categories according to their educational experiences.

$**df=2$, $p \leq .01$

Certainly, a high rate of truancy or suspension from school does not promote academic achievement (e.g. Ekstrom et al 1987) however, there may be a threshold at which these behaviors become a problem. Data collected on the High School Dropout informants revealed that 89% reported skipping school and were often chronic truants. Only 39.2% of the High School Student and 50% of the College Student informants reported ever skipping class. Due to a change in the response format we cannot tell how frequently they did so in comparison to the High School Droput informants, nonetheless, since the overall incidence of truancy decreases dramatically at the High School Student and College Student levels in comparison to the High School Dropout level, we may conclude that the frequency of the truancy is also diminished.

The three groups of informants also differed in their leisure activities (see Table 10). High School Dropout informants appeared less productive of all of the groups in the way in which they spent their free time. High School Dropout informants were the least likely of all three groups to engage in school-sponsored extracurricular activities, study for class, or even socialize with friends. High School Student informants participated in those activities to an increased degree over that of High School Dropout informants. College Student informants, however, were the most consistent in participating in extracurricular activities, studying and socializing with friends. Over 90% of College Student informants reported engaging in these activities during their free time.

Table 10. Percentage of informants reporting on different free time activities while attending high school.

	High School Dropouts %	High School Students %	College Students %	N	Chi-squared
Extracurricular Activities	39.5	44.7	94.4	178.6	30.857*
Studying	57.9	70.7	97.2	225.8	10.657*
Socializing with friends	68.4	93.6	91.7	253.7	4.657 (ns)

*df = 2, p≤.01

Research on dropouts indicates that less successful students report an overall dissatisfaction with school and as a result, do not participate to a great degree in extracurricular activities, do not spend time studying, and instead engage in social activities with their friends (e.g. Ekstrom et al 1987). Although few (7.9%) High School Dropout informants in this sample stated that they dropped out because they didn't like school, High School Dropout informants overall did indeed exhibit a diminished degree of studying and participation in school related extracurricular activities. Curiously however, the High School Dropout informants seem isolated, not only from school environment, but also from other social environments (e.g. family, friends) that for High School Student and College Student informants seem to be beneficial. Thus, while the participation in extracurricular activities and time spent studying may be related to academic achievement, the types and frequencies of social interaction and their impact on academic achievement of Hispanic youth warrant further investigation.

Only 28.9% of High School Dropout informants and 23.9% of High School Student informants reported working while in high school; data for College Student informants was omitted in error. Nonetheless, given that less than 30% of the High School Dropout informants reported working while in high school suggests that there is little relationship between high school employment and leaving school. Still, this variable is still a valid area of study for future research since Rumberger (1983), whose results yielded neither a positive nor a negative impact of work on Hispanic academic achievement, conflicts with Valdivieso's (1986) findings of a negative impact of employment on Hispanic youths' education. Moreover, the impact of the number of hours worked per week on academic achievement (Steinberg et al 1982) needs to be validated for Hispanic populations.

The percentages of positive attitudes towards one's self was high for all groups, confirming Valdivieso's (1986) contention that these measures are not culturally applicable to Hispanic populations. Informants at higher academic levels displayed a slightly more positive attitudinal outlook of themselves. As Table 11 demonstrates, positive levels of self-esteem and feelings of competency increased slightly but steadily along with academic level. High School Student and College Student informants were also more likely than High School Dropout informants to attribute success to hard work rather than luck and, were less likely to feel that their progress was being hindered by persons or circumstances beyond their control.

Table 11. Percentage of informants reporting on attitudes toward oneself while attending high school.

	High School Dropouts %	High School Students %	College Students %
Positive attitude about self	76.3	82.5	91.7
As capable as others	84.2	88.8	94.4
Work more important than luck	73.7	86.7	83.3
Others stopping you	50.0	21.8	27.8*

*$(2, N = 99.6) = 13.294$, $p \leq .01$

Informants from higher academic levels, then, displayed an increased degree of confidence over their counterparts that had dropped out from school. On the other hand, the lesser degree of positive responses made by the High School Dropout informants serve to reiterate the lesser degree of confidence felt by the High School Dropout informants overall. Moreover, clearly half of the High School Dropout informants felt that they were not in full control of their own destiny, a trait that previous research (e.g. Ekstrom et al 1987) cited as common among dropouts.

While improved student behaviors and self-esteem accompanied higher levels of academic achievement, the degree of support students received from their parents was also related to their academic level. High School Dropout informants were less than half as likely than High School Student and College Student students to receive help from their parents on homework. Furthermore High School Dropout parents were less likely to engage in discussions with their children regarding their post-high school plans. Parents of the College Student and High School Student informants were also much more likely than the parents of the High School Dropout informants to know the whereabouts of their child during non-school hours (see Table 12). These results provide evidence of a stronger familial connection for individuals at higher academic levels and is characteristic of the high degree of parental support that previous research (e.g. Ekstrom et al 1987) has identified as important to a student's academic success.

Table 12. Percentage of informants receiving support from parents.

	High School Dropouts %	High School Students %	College Students %	N	Chi-squared
Help with homework	21.1	54.3	44.4	119.8	14.550*
Discuss future plans	47.4	87.2	86.1	220.7	13.968*
Location of informant	55.3	85.1	97.2	237.6	11.742*

*df = 2, p≤.01

To summarize, factors such as the incidence of retention, suspension and low grade point average were the academic variables seen here to be strong indicators of dropping out. The track in which students were enrolled while in high school also seemed to moderately influence academic achievement, suggesting that placement in a vocational track rather than an academic or at least general track, does not encourage students to remain in school.

College Student informants exhibited a more positive attitude toward the school environment over High School Student and High School Dropout informants as evidenced by their higher degree of participation in extracurricular activities and higher reported degree of studying. These results suggest that these factors can also be considered indicators of academic achievement. Regarding other non-school activities it was noted that High School Student and College Student informants reported a higher degree of time spent socializing with friends than did High School Dropout informants. This result suggests that, contrary to Ekstrom et al (1987), increased socialization could aid in forging a positive social environment and thus may be beneficial to academic achievement within the Midwestern Mexican community. However, additional research is needed to confirm this suggestion.

4.3 SOCIOLINGUISTIC PROFILE

A comparison of the sociolinguistic profiles of the informants from all three groups yielded an overall positive association between academic achievement and Spanish. Several language use measures showed an increased incorporation of Spanish as academic level rose, indicating that Spanish is not a hindrance to academic achievement among Midwestern Mexican youths, contrary to popular assumption. Likewise, several attitude measures recorded responses where increases in their appraisal of Spanish went along with academic level, indicating that strong cultural ties to Spanish were also not a hindrance to academic achievement.

Finally, informants from this study were seen to exhibit language use and language attitude characteristics that were different from the traits seen in Southwest Mexican populations. Attitudes expressed toward Spanish and English indicated a trend toward the utilization of both languages rather than a shift toward either Spanish or English alone. Similarly, informants in this study were seen to attribute an *instrumental* value to Spanish as well as to English suggesting that, for Midwestern Mexican populations, both languages are viewed as economic assets.

Regarding their first language, informants from all categories reported that they were more likely to have learned to speak Spanish as their first language, an occurrence consistent with the recency of immigration noted among informants. Reading and writing skills, however, were most frequently learned first in English (see Table 13). The data did reveal, however, that High School Dropout informants, only 55.3% of whom were born in the U.S., were much more likely than High School Student or College Student informants to learn to speak, read and write in English alone rather than in Spanish alone or in combination with English. That is, informants at higher levels of academic achievement reported an increased exposure to Spanish alone or in combination with English than informants at lower levels. These findings suggest that exposure to Spanish seems to have aided the informants' academic attainment.

Given the high numbers of informants that indicated they had acquired their literacy skills in English, it is not surprising to see that High School Dropout, High School Student and College Student were all somewhat uniform in their perception of their own proficiency in English. The vast majority of the informants in all three groups rated their English skills as either "Excellent" or "Well" (see Table 14).[3] Overall, informants from all categories displayed a high degree of confidence in their abilities first to understand English, and next to read in that language, then speak and write. This suggests that informants were, in general, more confident in their comprehension than in their

Table 13. Percentage of informants reporting first language skills in Spanish and English.

	High School Dropouts %	High School Students %	College Students %	N	Chi-squared
First Language Spoken					
Spanish	50.0	62.8	69.4	182.2	3.203 (ns)
English	44.7	12.2	5.6	62.5	42.057*
Both	5.3	23.4	25.0	53.7	13.375*
First Language Read					
Spanish	23.7	33.5	27.8	100.0	80.004*
English	73.7	42.6	61.1	97.9	6.663**
Both	2.6	21.8	11.1	35.5	15.644*
First Language Written					
Spanish	23.7	31.9	27.8	83.4	1.209 (ns)
English	71.1	43.0	61.1	175.2	6.947**
Both	5.3	22.9	11.1	39.3	12.280*

*df = 2, p≤.01

**df = 2, p≤.05

production of English. Additionally, it was noted that College Student informants, perhaps due to their greater academic experience, rated themselves slightly higher than High School Dropout and High School Student informants in their abilities to understand, read, and write in English.

The informants' consistently high ranking of their abilities in English suggest that relatively few of the informants at any level perceived themselves as having any deficiencies in their English language skills. When these results are considered in light of the information presented in Tables 13 (previously) and 15 (to follow), it appears that exposure to Spanish did not diminish the informants' confidence in their English abilities.

The informants' responses regarding their Spanish skills, however, were much lower indicating that informants at all levels were much less confident in their abilities in Spanish than in their abilities in English (see Table 15). Overall, High School Dropout informants were seen to have the lowest perception of their Spanish abilities in all of the four

Table 14. Percentage of informants reporting their English skills as "Excellent" or "Well".*

	High School Dropouts %	High School Students %	College Students %
Speaking	89.5	85.6	88.9
Understanding	92.1	91.5	97.2
Reading	89.5	88.3	94.4
Writing	84.2	87.8	88.9

*None of the chi-squared comparisons were significant.

skills with barely half ranking their abilities to speak and understand as at least "Well". Furthermore, High School Dropout informants expressed much less confidence in their written skills than in their oral skills in Spanish.

By comparison, High School Student informants, ranked themselves consistently higher than the High School Dropout informants in their Spanish abilities in all four skill areas with more than half of the High School Student informants ranking their skills in all areas as either "Excellent" or "Well". Still, High School Student informants felt more comfortable about their oral skills than their written skills.

Responses for College Student informants were generally higher than those of the other two groups. In contrast to the High School Dropout and High School Student informants however, College Student informants tended to favor their comprehension skills (reading and understanding) over their production skills (speaking and writing). This difference may be due to their exposure to a standard Spanish at the university.[4] Nonetheless, it was noted that higher levels of education were accompanied by a higher degree of confidence in one's ability to speak, understand, read and write Spanish.

The results of the Spanish vocabulary measure revealed that most High School Student and College Student informants scored very highly, indicating that, overall, the Spanish proficiency of High School Student and College Student informants was high.[5] The Spanish vocabulary measure was seen to correlate positively, though moderately, with the informants' self-reported proficiency in Spanish. However, a graphic analysis of the data revealed that although vocabulary scores were very high, both High School Student and

Table 15. Informants reporting their Spanish skills as "Excellent" or "Well".

	High School Dropouts %	High School Students %	College Students %	*N*	Chi-squared
Speaking	50.0	71.8	69.4	191.2	4.484 (ns)
Understanding	55.3	83.5	88.9	227.7	8.578*
Reading	39.5	60.1	72.2	171.8	9.546**
Writing	23.7	52.1	52.8	128.6	12.860**

*df = 2, p≤.05

**df = 2, p≤.01

College Student informants were hesitant in rating their Spanish skills by using the highest of the four terms ("Excellent") and instead, favored the second highest term ("Well"). Thus, the lower magnitude of correlation was primarily due to the informants' underestimate of their own language skills.

In sum, the consistency of the self-ranking of English skills for all three groups of informants suggests that informants at all academic levels generally feel confident of their abilities in English. Confidence in Spanish abilities was seen to vary somewhat within groups according to the skill involved (i.e. comprehension/production; oral/written) in addition to varying between groups. The Spanish vocabulary measure, however, confirmed that the proficiency level of the High School Student and College Student informants was high overall.

These data suggest, then, that Spanish does not act as a hindrance to academic achievement of the Midwest Mexican informants in this study. Moreover, an exclusive or heightened early exposure to English is also not related to higher levels of academic achievement among these informants. The sections that follow present the summaries of the information regarding language use and language attitudes.

4.3.1 Language use

Informants from all academic levels reported conversing with a number of interlocutors, however, the average number of family and friends with whom informants interacted increased along academic lines. The 38 High School Dropout informants reported interacting with a total of 278 interlocutors (mean = 7.3); the 188 High School Student informants interacted with 1979 interlocutors (for a mean of 10.5 per informant); College Student informants interacted with 417 interlocutors (yielding a mean of 11.6 interlocutors per informant). It thus appears that as informants increased in academic level, the more they interacted with those around them, perhaps reflective of their higher degrees of confidence they expressed in their language abilities. High School Dropout informants, on the other hand, appear to be more isolated.

In examining the patterns of language chosen for conversations with different interlocutors, three trends were noted. First, the language informants reported choosing for conversation was often seen to match the informants' perception of the interlocutor's language proficiency. That is to say, that when the informant perceived the interlocutor as being more dominant in Spanish, s/he spoke to that individual more in Spanish. Likewise, conversations were more often conducted in English when the informant indicated that the interlocutor was more dominant in that language.

Language choice was seen to be associated with two other factors related to the interlocutor: place of birth and age difference to informant. These factors were more clearly associated language choice than were interlocutor age or kinship relation alone. Regarding place of birth, informants at all levels were much more likely to engage Mexican born interlocutors in conversations in Spanish rather than English. Similarly English conversations were much more likely to be carried out with interlocutors who were born in the United States.

Regarding the age difference between informant and interlocutor, a general pattern of language use was somewhat regular across the informants of different academic levels. Though the boundaries of the stages are varied between High School Dropout, High School Student and College Student informants, a general pattern does emerge (see Table 16). In the pattern, Spanish is seen to dominate as the language of conversation with older interlocutors. Next is noted a transition to balancing conversations rather evenly between Spanish and English with the next group of interlocutors, still older than the informant, but younger than the first group of interlocutors. English dominates conversations with interlocutors that are around the same age as the informant, including interlocutors that fall into both older and younger age groups than the informant. Lastly, a renewed use of Spanish is noted with the youngest interlocutors.[6]

Table 16. General pattern of language choice according to age difference between informant and interlocutor.

	High School Students	High School Students	College Students
Language of Conversation			
Spanish	>25 yrs older	>15 yrs older	>20 yrs older
Spanish or English	10-24 yrs older	5-14 yrs older	15-19 yrs older
English	9 yrs older to 10 yrs younger	4 yrs older to 10 yrs younger	14 yrs older to 15 yrs younger
Spanish	>11 yrs younger	>11 yrs younger	>16 yrs younger

The consistency of the general pattern seen in Table 16 suggests that this is the overall pattern of language choice for the youths in the Chicago area. Moreover, since it is somewhat consistent, it suggests that the use of Spanish that is incorporated in the daily lives of the informants does not hinder academic achievement.

This notion is reinforced in Table 17. High School Dropout informants, the least academically successful, were the informants who reported conducting the highest percentage ($127 \div 278 = 45.7\%$) of their total conversations exclusively in English. High School Student and College Student informants, respectively, used English exclusively with only 18.7% and 21.3% of their interlocutors. For High School Student informants, the most frequently chosen language for conversation was Spanish, employed exclusively with 26.8% of their interlocutors. College Student informants reported "mostly English", as their most frequent language choice (30.5%), but this may be an influence of the environment in which they live and were interviewed. That is, since neither the university community of which they are a part nor the twin cities that surround the campus present a bilingual environment, the College Student students' responses may have been skewed toward English to a higher degree than for the other two groups who were interviewed in Chicago. Overall, however, from the increased use of Spanish and decreased emphasis on exclusively using English among informants at higher academic levels one can conclude that Spanish use for communication purposes is not a hindrance to academic achievement.

Table 17. Frequency totals for Language Choice for interpersonal communication.*

| | LANGUAGE CHOICE | | | | | |
	Only Span.	Mostly Span.	Both Equally	Mostly Eng.	Only Eng.	Total
High School Dropout Total	58	23	39	31	**127**	278
High School Student Total	**508**	338	437	255	354	1892
College Student Total	82	38	72	**122**	85	399

*Some interlocutors were not included due to incomplete information.

As mentioned above, High School Dropout, High School Student and College Student informants displayed a somewhat consistent pattern in their language use for interactions with family and friends. However, the data regarding the informants' personal language use (i.e. for receptive, internal, emotional and purposeful language) were very different across groups (see Table 18).

Spanish alone was not favored by any of the groups. However, an increase in a preference for the use of Spanish, either in combination with English or as an equal to English was noted to increase along with the academic level of the informants. In general, High School Dropout informants preferred English for all four language purposes. High School Student preferred both languages for oral receptive purposes, and codeswitching for emotional and purposeful language. High School Student preferred English alone only for reading and internal language. College Student informants preferred both languages for oral receptive and internal language and English only for reading. College Student informants preferred codeswitching for emotional language and for purposeful language as an alternate to English. While no group of informants favored using Spanish alone for their personal language contexts, informants at higher academic levels are seen to frequently incorporate Spanish as part of their personal language. These results again suggest that Spanish use is not a hindrance to academic achievement. On the contrary, it appears that Spanish may aid academic achievement.

Table 18. Language most favored for Receptive, Internal, Emotional and Purposeful Language.

	High School Dropouts %	High School Students %	College Students %
Receptive			
Oral	English	Both	Both
(TV, music)	(68.4%)	(47.3%)	(55.6%)
Written	English	English	English
(books, magazines)	(81.6%)	(65.1%)	(57.4%)
Internal Language	English	English	Both
(thinking, praying)	(63.2%)	(46.9%)	(44.4%)
Emotional*	English	Codeswitching	Codeswitching
(when angry, nervous)	(48.0%)	(44.4%)	(44.4%)
Purposeful* (explaining, arguing)	English	Codeswitching	Codeswitching /English
	(60.2%)	(40.6%)	(32.9%/32.5%)

*High School Dropout informants were provided with the options of Only Spanish, Mostly Spanish, Both Equally, Mostly English, and Only English. Options for High School Student and College Student informants were: "Spanish," "English," "Both," and "Mixed Spanish and English"

Regarding the *appropriateness* of language for specific topics, it was noted that informants felt overall that both languages, that is, either Spanish or English, were appropriate for a variety of topics (see Table 19). Nonetheless, many topics also showed a tendency toward one language or the other and informants from the three academic levels allocated their preferences differently.

While informants from all groups approved of both Spanish and English as appropriate for most topics, tendency toward one language or another was seen to be associated with academic level. High School Dropout informants were seen to largely favor English while the High School Student and College Student informants tended toward English to a successively less degree. For example, neither High School Dropout nor High School Student informants felt comfortable including Spanish as a language equal to English for the two most formal topics, *science* and *military commands.* College Student informants, on the

Table 19. Appropriateness of language for specific topics.*

	High School Dropouts	High School Students	College Students
Language(s)			
English Only	science, military commands	science, military commands	none
Both, tending toward English	politics, novels, poetry, folksongs, bargaining, jokes, cursing, lying, persuading	politics, novels, poetry, folksongs, lying, persuading	science, military commands, lying
Both	religious rituals, baby talk	jokes, cursing	politics, bargaining, jokes, cursing, persuading
Both, tending toward Spanish	none	religious rituals, baby talk	religious rituals, novels, poetry, folksongs, baby talk

other hand, did not classify any of the given topics as appropriate only for English. Rather, College Student informants felt that either language would be an appropriate choice, even for *science* and *military commands,* though there was still a tendency to favor English. Even so, this slight tendency toward English may be due to the monolingual English environment in which they were interviewed.

The reverse tendency was also observed. High School Dropout informants did not tend toward Spanish on any of the topics, however, the tendency to incorporate Spanish was seen to increase to a successive degree as academic level rose. Furthermore, College Student informants did not appear to prefer one language over the other for more formal situations rather the selection of "Both" with a tendency toward English included both formal and informal topics as did the selection of "Both" with a tendency toward Spanish. In general then, informants at higher academic levels were seen to be more willing to incorporate Spanish in a wider variety of contexts. Moreover, informants at the highest academic level to view both Spanish and

English as appropriate for both formal and informal topics. These results again suggest that Spanish use is not a hindrance to academic achievement.

In sum, informants at all three levels were seen to employ similar criteria for their interpersonal language use. In general the use of Spanish or English for conversations for all three groups of informants was guided by the perception of the language proficiency of the interlocutor, the interlocutor's place of birth, the age difference between the interlocutor and informant. High School Dropout informants were known to utilize the most English for their conversations while High School Student informants were known to use Spanish to the highest degree. College Student informants reported conducting more conversations in English than in Spanish, however, it was suggested that the emphasis on English in the university environment where these informants were surveyed may have influenced these responses. The topic of conversation in interpersonal interactions was seen as having a small influence over language choice, however, further investigation is needed before firm conclusions can be drawn.

A greater incorporation of Spanish in personal language (i.e. receptive, internal, emotional, and purposeful), was seen to occur as academic level rose. Similarly, an increase in academic level accompanied a view of Spanish as an appropriate language for a broader number of topics. These results demonstrate that Spanish continues to be used to a high degree by Mexicans in Chicago, both as a medium for interpersonal exchanges as well as a means of personal communication. Moreover, the results overwhelmingly suggest that Spanish does not interfere with academic achievement. Instead, it again appears that increased Spanish use benefits those at higher academic levels.

4.3.2 Language attitudes

The responses to the various attitude measures revealed that informants from all three academic levels held largely positive attitudes toward Spanish. These results serve to reinforce the notion that Spanish is an important part of the community as a whole. Interestingly, however, informants also often expressed positive attitudes about English to a similar degree, indicating that their high regard for Spanish was not to the exclusion of English nor vice-versa.

It was further noted that the greatest degree of comfort and acceptance of Spanish was expressed by informants at the highest academic level. These results indicate that strong cultural ties to Spanish do not hinder the academic progress of Mexican youths in the Midwest.

As seen in Table 20, the means of the informants' responses to the *semantic differential* demonstrate that informants hold generally positive attitudes toward Spanish. Moreover, a comparison of the means across groups for each item reveals a nearly consistent increase in positive feelings toward Spanish along academic lines. The exceptions to this trend are the items *logical, sophisticated, public,* and *superior.* Similar to the results observed for language use variables, the responses to the *semantic differential* suggest that highly positive views of Spanish can be maintained without registering any detriment to academic achievement.

Table 20. Means of responses to items on the *semantic differential* regarding Spanish.*

	High School Dropouts	High School Students	College Students	Grand Means (rows)
Pretty	3.97	4.44	4.80	4.40
Rich	3.50	4.06	4.57	4.04
Musical	3.32	3.72	4.06	3.70
Precise	3.34	3.72	4.47	3.84
Logical	3.66	3.65	4.26	3.86
Sophisticated	2.95	2.62	3.51	3.03
Rhythmic	3.42	3.91	4.29	3.87
Refined	3.55	3.76	4.14	3.82
Colorful	3.63	3.76	4.57	3.99
Public	3.32	3.59	3.54	3.48
Superior	3.34	3.89	3.37	3.53
Pure	3.26	3.86	4.17	3.76
Soothing	3.29	3.81	4.17	3.76
Graceful	3.63	4.21	4.31	4.05
Sacred	3.29	3.04	3.74	3.36
Grand Means (columns)	3.43	3.74	4.13	

*Values here may range from a low of 1 (very negative) to a high of 5 (very positive).

Responses to the statements regarding *affective* attitudes recorded increases in positive feelings toward Spanish along academic level (see Table 21). Increases in feeling *proud*, feeling *lucky* and feeling that it is *important to speak Spanish* were seen to accompany a rise in academic level. Informants of all groups, however, are reticent in stating that they prefer to speak Spanish rather than English, as well as the inverse. This hesitance was particularly noted in the case of College Student informants, however, was less strong in the case of the High School Dropout informants.

A high positive *affective* attitude was noted for English as well, though in many cases not as high as Spanish. The overall pattern of responses indicated that High School Dropout informants consistently rated English higher than Spanish. The reverse was true for High School Student and College Student informants who, in almost all cases, rated Spanish higher than English. In general then, while the positive attitudes favor both languages, informants' attitudes of an *affective* nature toward Spanish rise, dramatically in some instances, along with academic level. This indicates that students at higher levels of academic achievement retain strong and positive *affective* feelings toward Spanish.

Table 21. Percentage of informants who responded "Agree" to *affective* statements.

	Spanish			English		
	High School Dropouts %	High School Students %	College Students %	High School Dropouts %	High School Students %	College Students %
AFFECTIVE						
Prefer to speak . . .	15.8	14.9	16.7	47.4	19.2	8.3*
Proud to speak . . .	71.1	87.8	94.4	89.5	81.9	77.8
Lucky to speak . . .	68.4	73.4	91.7	73.7	70.7	83.3
Important to you to speak . . .	73.7	90.9	100.0	97.4	92.0	97.2

*(2, N = 74.9) = 32.615, p≤.01

Similar to previous research (e.g. Elías-Olivares 1976b, Hurtado & Gurín 1987, Galindo 1991), were the responses to the items measuring *instrumental* attitudes (see Table 22). A high percentage of informants across all three groups provided affirmative responses for all items except *more educated if speak;* responses for this item were somewhat lower across all informant groups. Overall, these results suggest that the *instrumental* value of English is not associated with any one academic level. That is, the fact that all three groups attributed a highly utilitarian value to English indicates that informants at all three academic levels recognize English as a tool for communication and progress, a fact which confirms the findings of previous research.

Clearly contrary to previous research (e.g. Elías-Olivares 1976b), however, informants here, particularly the College Student informants, indicated they felt that Spanish bore an *instrumental* value. The percentage of responses were generally high, indicating that all groups of informants felt an instrumental association with Spanish. However, responses for one item, *more educated if speak* , were low indicating that informants did not seem to associate either Spanish or English with degree of education.

In general then, the results indicate that similar to previous research (e.g. Elías-Olivares 1976b), an *instrumental* value is associated with English for all groups suggesting that the utilitarian value of English is not at issue for informants at any academic level. Interestingly however, an *instrumental* value is also attributed to Spanish at a similar degree. Additionally, it was noted that informants at higher academic levels more readily associated an *instrumental* value to Spanish. These results reveal that individuals at higher academic levels recognized the economic benefits of bilingualism and further stress the notion that ties to Spanish are not detrimental to academic achievement.

Responses to the items measuring *integrative* attitudes revealed an overall steady increases in attributing *integrative* values to Spanish as academic level rose; responses toward English, however, were more mixed. All items, with the exception of *more at ease with those who speak . . .* , demonstrated steady increases along academic levels. The excepted item showed roughly even degree of responses across all levels. Nonetheless, the increasingly *integrative* feelings associated with Spanish indicate that informants at higher academic levels do not

Table 22. Percentage of informants who responded "Agree" to *instrumental* **items**

	Spanish			English		
	High School Dropouts %	High School Students %	College Students %	High School Dropouts %	High School Students %	College Students %
INSTRUMENTAL						
More work if speak . . .	68.4	74.5	100.0*	89.5	77.7	83.3
Can communicate more if speak . . .	73.7	71.3	97.2	76.3	73.9	88.9
It is useful to know . . .	92.1	85.6	100.0	97.4	86.7	97.2
More educated if speak . . .	47.4	55.3	61.1	57.9	52.7	61.1

*(2, N = 242.9) = 6.941, p≤.05

Table 23. Percentage of informants who responded "Agree" to *integrative* **items.**

	Spanish			English		
	High School Dropouts %	High School Students %	College Students %	High School Dropouts %	High School Students %	College Students %
INTEGRATIVE						
More at ease with those who speak . . .	52.6	46.8	52.8	57.9	39.4	38.9
More friends if speak . . .	42.1	44.6	50.0	68.4	50.5	58.3
Feel like part of group speaking . . .	39.5	42.5	55.6	23.7	28.2	38.9
. . . is important to family life	63.2	83.5	91.7	52.6	43.1	38.9
. . . is important to school life	26.3	47.3	80.6*	89.5	76.6	94.4
. . . is important to social life	47.7	59.6	83.3*	81.6	64.9	86.1

*school life: (2, N = 154.2) = 29.172, p≤.01; social life: (2, N = 190.6) = 10.339, p≤.01

feel uncomfortable as members of a linguistically distinct group and can furthermore interact as such in both informal (e.g. family) settings as well as formal (e.g. school) settings.

Responses to the items measuring *integrative* attitudes toward English are more varied. Affirmative responses to two items, *more at ease with those who speak . . .* , and *. . . is important to family life*, declined as academic level rose. Interestingly, positive responses to one item, *feel like part of a group speaking . . .* , rose along with academic level, however the level of response did not reach that of the same item regarding Spanish. Responses for the remaining items, *more friends if speak . . . , . . . is important to school life*, and *. . . is important to social life*, were mixed with High School Student informants less convinced of the *integrative* nature of English than either the High School Dropout or College Student informants.

These results indicate that informants increase in *integrative* feelings toward Spanish as they increase in academic level. *Integrative* feelings toward English, on the other hand, seem to be more complex. Still, the consistency of the pattern regarding *integrative* attitudes toward Spanish emphasizes again, that informants in this study did not feel the need to sacrifice their ties with Latino culture in order to succeed academically.

Responses to the items regarding *language loyalty* revealed mixed results (see Table 24). Responses toward Spanish were noted as being high overall, but did not necessarily follow a pattern according to academic level. Similarly, responses to English were high, but neither increased nor diminished along academic lines. In general, College Student informants affirmed their loyalty to Spanish to a higher degree than did either of the other two groups, while High School Dropout informants displayed the highest degree of loyalty toward English. High School Student informants, on the other hand, often displayed the lowest degree of loyalty toward either language.

Three items referring to Spanish, *. . . helps community progress, Spanish is important part of Latino culture,* and *Want children to know Spanish,* drew some of the strongest positive responses across all groups, and increased slightly with academic level. Informants also felt somewhat strongly that bilingual education was more appropriate as a medium for Latinos to learn English than for either Latinos or non-Latinos to learn Spanish, although High School Student informants were more moderate in their feelings toward bilingual education.

Table 24. Percentage of informants who responded "Agree" to *language loyalty* **items.**

	Spanish			English		
	High School Dropouts %	High School Students %	College Students %	High School Dropouts %	High School Students %	College Students %
LANGUAGE LOYALTY						
Bilingual Ed. should teach Latinos . . .	71.1	65.4	86.1	92.1	75.5	91.7
Latinos should know . . .	78.9	72.3	77.8	94.7	69.2	72.2
. . . helps community progress	71.1	71.3	94.4	89.5	69.2	75.0

	High School Dropouts %	High School Students %	College Students %
Spanish is important part of Latino culture	81.6	82.9	97.2
English is a threat to Latino culture	10.5	23.4	11.1*
Want children to know Spanish	78.9	90.4	100.0
Bilingual Ed. to promote Spanish for all	78.9	61.7	77.8

*(2, $N = 45.0$) = 7.068, p≤.05

Finally, community progress was seen to be aided by English more strongly by High School Dropout informants and to a lesser degree by High School Student and College Student informants.

The mixed responses to the items measuring *language loyalty* reveal that Mexican youths in the Midwest retain a loyalty to both Spanish and English. Overall, however, College Student informants displayed the highest loyalty to Spanish while High School Dropout informants were somewhat more loyal to English; High School Student informants were more moderate in their responses. Still, the percentage of positive responses to all of the items for both languages indicates that informants carry strong loyalties for both languages.

In sum, while the Midwestern Mexican youths in this study all appeared to express favorable attitudes toward Spanish, strong positive attitudes were also recorded for English. These results emphasize that the Midwestern Mexican youth culture is one that prefers the use of both languages rather than favor one over the other.

Informants in this study also revealed they attributed a strong *instrumental* value to Spanish as well as to English. While previous studies with Southwest populations have found that informants tend to attribute English with an *instrumental* value, extending those attributes to include Spanish is a result not found in the associating Spanish with an *instrumental* value has not been found in any earlier studies regarding the language attitudes of Mexican populations.

It should be again noted that while the College Student informants displayed the strongest feelings toward Spanish, they are the group at the highest academic level, thus their achievement has not suffered as a result of their positive attitudes toward Spanish. Conversely, diminished feelings toward Spanish do not appear to accompany a high degree of academic achievement.

4.6 CONCLUSION

The comparison of the results from the informants at three separate academic levels revealed that many indicators traditionally cited in the literature are not accurate predictors of academic achievement of Mexicans in the Midwest. In the present study, the most salient sociodemographic indicator of an informant's academic outcome appears to be sibling education. Parental occupational status and educational level also appear to influence academic achievement, but to a much more moderate degree. Factors such as family size and ethnic identity were not found to have any bearing on academic achievement.

From an academic standpoint, informants in the present study did conform more to characteristics found in the literature. Factors such as the incidence of retention, low grade point average and the incidence of suspension were found to be strong indicators of dropping out, while informants who lacked those features persisted in school. Participation in extracurricular activities and degree of time spent studying also appeared to play a minor role in staying in school, as noted in previous studies.

The track in which students were enrolled while in high school also seemed to be related to academic achievement, however, in a much more moderate sense than has been suggested in the literature. The data here seemed to suggest that placement in a vocational track, as opposed to an academic or general track, was least associated with academic achievement. Nonetheless, informants that studied in a general track in high school were not exempted from pursuing higher education. Thus, for the informants in the present study it appears that there are only two tracks: vocational and general/academic.

A comparison of the sociolinguistic profiles of the High School Dropout, High School Student and College Student informants revealed striking similarities across all groups. First, although informants at each level varied in the degree to which they reported using Spanish and English for interpersonal conversations, these interactions were guided by the same principles: the interlocutor's proficiency, the interlocutor's place of birth, and the interlocutor's age difference with respect to the informant. Second, regarding language attitudes, it was seen that informants at all academic levels exhibited generally positive attitudes toward Spanish. Still, many attitude measures also recorded positive feelings toward English indicating that the Midwest Mexican youths in this study held strong feelings toward the utilization and maintenance of both languages. The consistency of these characteristics across academic levels suggests that neither Spanish language use nor positive attitudes toward Spanish have interfered with the academic progress of the informants.

The informants did differ sociolinguistically across academic groups, but in ways which favored Spanish. First, an increased use of Spanish for personal language was associated with informants at higher academic levels, suggesting that the personal use of Spanish did not represent an academic hindrance. Likewise, College Student informants displayed the strongest positive feelings toward Spanish, and often did so unanimously. These result not only indicate the strong cultural and linguistic ties of the informants at the college level, they also demonstrate that maintaining such ties was not an obstacle to these informants' academic pursuits.

Thus, no evidence was found to support the claim that either the maintenance of Spanish or the cultural ties that are associated with the language is detrimental to academic achievement. On the contrary, the fact that informants at higher academic levels more often had an early exposure to Spanish literacy, expressed a greater confidence in their abilities in Spanish, reported incorporating Spanish to a greater extent in their personal lives and were the most adamant in their positive attitudes toward Spanish indicates that rather than act as an obstacle to education, Spanish may instead contribute positively to the academic achievement of Midwest Mexican youths.

NOTES

1. The term "Latino" is growing in popularity over "Hispanic" on the University of Illinois campus. It is likely that this sentiment influenced the selection of this term.

2. Due to uneven sample sizes, percentages were used in lieu of raw frequencies to calculate the chi-squared analyses in this chapter.

3. The four options provided were: "Excellent", "Well", "Fair", and "Poor".

4. Nine (25.0%) of the College Student informants were Spanish majors and others, while not majors, were surveyed during a basic Spanish language class. Others may have been recommended for participation in the study by their basic level Spanish teachers in exchange for extra credit points. While Spanish majors may be predisposed to positive attitudes toward Spanish and display a higher degree of Spanish use, the same profile cannot be assumed regarding the remaining 75% of informants.

5. This measure was incorporated into the survey instrument after data had already been collected on High School Dropout informants, therefore, similar data is not available for High School Dropout informants.

6. High School Dropout informants did speak primarily English with the interlocutors that were 11-20 years younger than themselves, however, because there was an increase in Spanish usage noted, they are included here.

CHAPTER 5

Mexicans, Spanish and Academic Success

Latinos are recognized as one of the youngest and fastest growing segments of the U.S. population. Nonetheless, this portion of the nation's population is burdened by a 45% annual high school dropout rate. While the factors underlying the dropout epidemic are complex, the status of Latinos as the nation's largest linguistic minority has invited criticism alluding to a language barrier that Latinos must overcome in order to succeed academically.

The present study focused on the individuals of one Latino national origin, Mexican, who comprise two-thirds of the nation's Latino population and account for a similar proportion of the Latino high school dropouts each year. Moreover, the informants in this study reside in the Midwest, an area that has received little attention from sociolinguistic researchers. The present study sought to both document the sociolinguistic attributes of the Mexican youth of the Midwest as well as explore the link between these sociolinguistic features and academic achievement. The major findings of the study, which have consequences for both sociolinguistic as well as educational disciplines, can be summarized as follows.

5.1 THE HETEROGENEITY OF MEXICAN POPULATIONS

The Midwest Mexican population is concentrated in a smaller geographic area than the corresponding population of the Southwest. Additionally, Solé (1990) revealed that the immigrant composition is different: 44% of the Mexican population of the Midwest is of a first generation status as opposed to less than 20% of those living in the Southwest. In addition to being both geographically and demographically distinct, the results of the present study revealed that Midwest Mexican informants displayed distinct patterns of use of Spanish and held somewhat different linguistic attitudes.

The language choice of Mexican populations of the Southwest has been seen to be based on kinship relationships. That is, southwesterners report speaking Spanish to parents and grandparents and English to siblings. In the present study, language choice was not found to be related to kinship rather, a more revealing pattern was found with respect to the age difference between the informant and the interlocutor whether that person was a family member or bilingual friend. In general, informants here spoke Spanish with the oldest interlocutors; employed Spanish and English in a balanced fashion with the next oldest interlocutors; used English in conversations with the interlocutors that were closest in age to themselves; and used Spanish again to converse with the very young. Nonetheless, while this general pattern was consistent across academic levels, the age boundaries that defined each were different for informants of each academic category. This result was attributed to the different degrees of confidence and proficiency in Spanish displayed by informants at different academic levels. Informants who had dropped out of school were found to be less proficient and reported having less confidence in their Spanish language abilities and therefore when they engaged in conversations in Spanish, they did so with individuals of a restricted age range. Informants at higher academic levels, on the other hand, were found to communicate in Spanish with interlocutors over a broader range of ages.

The informant's estimation of the interlocutor's language proficiency was a key in selecting the language of conversation. This result is not surprising considering the bilingual community in which the informants live. Life in such a community daily interaction with individuals who possess different degrees of Spanish skills. Thus, the ability to accommodate one's speech to that of one's interlocutor is a skill that arises out of communicative necessity.

While this interpersonal communication was found to be bound by characteristics of interlocutors, i.e. age difference and language proficiency, other differences between the Midwest and Southwest were found with respect to the choice of language for personal use (e.g. reading, praying, etc.) and for analyzing which language was the most appropriate for a particular topic. Informants in studies in the Southwest generally report a preference for Spanish for home use and for discussing informal topics (e.g. family issues) while English is employed for more formal topics and for use in a more public sphere (e.g. school, bank, hospital or other public institution). Midwest informants displayed a distinct pattern.

In the present study, such functional and locational distinctions were not clearly discernible across all groups. With the exception of an overall trend observed toward the use of English for reading, there was *never* a case in which all three informant groups were found to coincide regarding the use of either Spanish or English. Instead, informants at different academic levels employed Spanish and English for different purposes. High School Dropout informants favored English to a high degree for their personal use, while High School Student and College Student informants increasingly favored the use of Spanish and English codeswitching or Spanish as an alternative to English. Regarding formality, High School Dropout and High School Student selected only the two most formal topics (*science* and *military commands*) as appropriate for English alone. The remainder of the topics on the scale (*politics, religious rituals, novels, poetry, folksongs, bargaining, persuading, lying, joking, cursing, baby talk),* showed an increasing acceptance of the use of Spanish, particularly as academic level rose. Thus, for these informants, academic level and language use are related.

With respect to language attitudes, Southwest populations hold Spanish in regard for more *affective* and *integrative* reasons, and maintain a sense of *loyalty* to Spanish. At the same time, English is favored solely for *instrumental* reasons for Southwest speakers. Informants in the present study displayed somewhat different attitudes toward both languages. First, in addition to recognizing the *instrumental* value of English, informants in the present study also favored English for *affective* and *integrative* reasons. Moreover these Midwest informants expressed *loyalty* to English. These attributes have not been seen in previous studies of Mexican populations.

Midwest informants paralleled Southwest Spanish speakers in their regard for Spanish for *affective* and *integrative* purposes and in their expression of *loyalty* toward the language. The Midwest informants differed, however, in their attributing an *instrumental* value toward Spanish. This is yet another value that Mexican populations had not previously revealed.

These last two findings may spring from the influence of residing in a Midwestern region. Chicago is an industrial capital with a long history of attracting large numbers of various immigrant groups. For these groups, English became the lingua franca. The city's location, far from the U.S.-Mexico border, has allowed Midwest Mexicans to be spared the depth of the linguistic and social repression that has characterized the history of the border region of the American Southwest. Thus, the greater contact with diverse immigrant groups as well as a reduced degree of linguistic repression has contributed to the acceptance of both English and Spanish as equal partners in the informants' linguistic repertoires.

Overall, these results point to the differences that arise due to regional and demographic differences between Mexican populations of the Southwest and Midwest that should be taken into consideration in further studies of Mexican communities. Moreover, the findings reveal that the academic achievement and the sociolinguistic characteristics of the informants are related. In this community, those individuals who are less able to utilize both languages are also less successful academically; those at a higher level of academic achievement are those who are more able to integrate themselves in and between two cultures and languages.

5.2 ACADEMIC INDICATORS OF ACADEMIC ACHIEVEMENT.

The literature on dropouts has identified several academic characteristics that point to leaving school. The strongest of these factors, i.e. GPA and grade retention, were confirmed here. High School Dropout informants were more likely to have obtained low grades in school and were much more likely to have been held back at some point in their academic career, and for a longer period of time, than were informants at higher academic levels. Incidences of these two factors steadily diminished as academic level increased.

Dropout studies also claim that the incidence of participation in extracurricular activities and time spent studying can predict academic outcomes. Confirmation of these factors was found in the present study. Informants increasingly reported spending free time participating in school-related activities and studying as academic level rose; over 90% of College Student informants reported regularly engaging in these two activities.

Another factor, high school track placement, has been cited in the literature as an important determinant of academic success; namely, that students in an academic track will attend college more often than those completing their high school degrees in a general or vocational track. In the present study there appeared to have been only a binary distinction, one of "vocational" vs. "non-vocational." Moreover, track placement was seen to have a more moderate influence than in other studies. Few (8.3%) of the College Student informants were enrolled in a vocational track in high school as opposed to over 21.8% High School Student and 23.7% of High School Dropout informants. Thus, the chances of college attendance among Mexicans of the Midwest is severely limited through the participation in a vocational track in high school. The chances for college attendance improve if the student is enrolled in a non-vocational curriculum. Unfortunately, schools continue to place disproportionate numbers of Latino students in vocational courses (Valdivieso 1986, O'Malley 1987). In order to slow the alarming Latino high school dropout rate, educational administrators must initiate changes to ensure that increasing numbers of Latino students will be placed in more academically challenging curriculums. Students need to enhance their scholarly acumen, not merely develop trade skills.

Other academic factors that have been cited in the literature, i.e. truancy, suspension, feeling that others were stopping one's progress and parental support, were found not to be accurate predictors of academic outcome as claimed in studies elsewhere (e.g. Ekstrom et al 1987). Still other factors such as socializing with friends, having a positive attitude about one's self, feeling as capable as others, and feeling good luck was more important than one's efforts, were found to have little bearing on the academic achievement of the informants in this study. Thus, these factors are of questionable utility for predicting the academic achievement of Mexican populations.

Moreover, while other factors, i.e. GPA, track placement, grade retention, extracurricular participation and studying, were found to be more accurate predictors of dropout, it should be emphasized that they only serve to mark the consequences of what one must imagine must have been a sequence of complex events that preceded that outcome. That is to say, a number of social and academic factors, (such as parental involvement, amount of studying), over the course of the informants' academic careers, ultimately contributed in their accumulating a particular grade point average, in being retained (or not) one or more grades, in being placed in a given academic track or in an attitude toward studying and a willingness (or not) to participate in school events. Thus, it is important to recognize that although GPA, grade retention, extracurricular participation and studying are more accurate predictors of academic achievement than are the other variables examined here, further study must be undertaken to discern the factors that underlie each of these indicators.

5.3 SOCIODEMOGRAPHIC INDICATORS OF ACADEMIC ACHIEVEMENT.

Literature on high school dropouts has traditionally relied upon sociodemographic factors such as ethnicity, large family size, low socioeconomic level, and low level of parental education as some of the strongest indicators of dropping out. In the present study, only one of these factors, the occupation of parents, particularly that of the fathers, appeared to be related to the informants' academic outcome. However, this factor was seen to be only marginally related to the academic achievement of the informants in this study.

With regard to the ethnicity, family size and parents' education, no influence was found. Informants at all three academic levels most frequently identified themselves as Mexican. Moreover, informants at all three levels were found to be comparable with respect to the size of their families and the level of education of their parents. As a result, not one of these factors was found to have any significant bearing on predicting the academic outcome of the informants in the present study.

The strongest sociodemographic indicator of academic achievement for the informants in the present study was found to be the level of sibling education. Only 8.3% of the College Student informants and 12.2% of the High School Student informants had siblings that had dropped out of high school. In contrast, 44.7% of High School Dropout informants reported that they also had siblings who had dropped out. College Student informants were nearly twice as likely as either High School Student or High School Dropout informants to have siblings with college experience. This result reveals that the informants here model their school efforts after those of the siblings that have come before them rather than after those of their parents. Thus, individuals who have dropout siblings are often challenged to be the first to succeed academically in their family. Moreover, these students have the added burden of attempting to succeed where others close to them have been known to fail. Once a sibling has broken through the threshold of college attendance, the quest for academic success is made more tangible for those who follow. Here, the answer seems clear: success begets success. If more Latinos are to reach higher levels of academic achievement in the future, efforts must be made to foster the success of those who are in school now.

In sum, while the sociodemographic characteristics cited in the dropout literature may be accurate indicators of academic achievement for the general student population across the U.S., they fail to discern any real differences between individuals within the Midwest Mexican community and as a consequence, lose their ability to predict educational outcomes among members of this particular population. That is to say, since the sociodemographic and academic characteristics of individual communities are lost when incorporated in studies done at a national level, the factors revealed by such studies often fail to predict dropping out of a given region. Therefore, research must be undertaken to identify sociodemographic characteristics which are both relevant to the Mexican population and accurate predictors of school-leaving. Furthermore, these studies must take into consideration the regional and linguistic influences that define the particular community being studied.

5.4 SPANISH DOES NOT HINDER ACADEMIC ACHIEVEMENT.

Despite the claims commonly made in educational literature, there was *no* evidence found in the present study to indicate that Spanish hindered the academic achievement of the informants. Informants who were enrolled in either high school or college were much more confident of their abilities to speak, understand, read and write in Spanish than were informants who had dropped out of school.

Similarly, with regard to language choice, High School Dropout informants, reported using English exclusively in 45% of their interactions with other people. By contrast, High School Student and College Student informants used English exclusively in only 21% and 18% (respectively) of their interpersonal conversations. Even more notable, informants reported employing Spanish more often in these personal activities as academic level rose as reported in 5.1 above. Considering that personal and interpersonal use of Spanish increases along with academic level provides evidence to counter the claim that Spanish is a barrier to academic achievement. Still, this evidence must be tempered with the knowledge that 25% of the College Student informants were majoring in Spanish.

Additionally, informants from all academic levels expressed favorable attitudes toward English. With the exception of 47.4% the High School Dropout informants preferring to speak English, fewer than 20% of the High School Student and College Student informants claimed a preference toward speaking either Spanish or English[1]; the remaining *affective* items revealed that English was regarded highly. On *instrumental* measures between 70% and 97% of the informants at all three academic levels recognized the value of English with respect to obtaining employment, being able to communicate with others, or simply as being a useful language to know. Between 69% and 94% of all informants expressed a high degree of *loyalty* toward both English and less than 24% viewed English as a threat to Latino culture. On *integrative* measures, responses were lower for both Spanish and English however, at least 64% of all informants attributed an *instrumental* value to English in the areas of school life and social life.

In general then, neither a high use of Spanish in personal and interpersonal instances was seen to impede academic achievement. Likewise, informants in the present study were seen to hold both languages in high regard with no apparent detriment to academic achievement. Thus, there is no support for the claim that Spanish hinders academic achievement.

5.5 EXPOSURE TO SPANISH IN A FORMAL ENVIRONMENT PROMOTES ACADEMIC ACHIEVEMENT.

In the present study, High School Student and College Student informants displayed higher levels of exposure to Spanish in a formal environment than were the High School Dropout informants. Nearly one-third of both the High School Student and College Student informants reported having been taught to read and write in Spanish first or simultaneously with English. In contrast, over 70% of the students at the lowest level of academic achievement reported learning to read and write in English alone. This fact may be related to the generational characteristics of the informants. While 65% of the High School Dropout informants had at least one parent who had been born abroad, over 80% of both High School Student and College Student informants reported one of their parents being foreign-born.

Additionally, High School Student informants were nearly twice as likely as the High School Dropout informants to have participated in bilingual education or Spanish-only curriculums, and College Student informants were two to three times as likely than High School Dropout informants to have participated in such programs. These results are important in that they not only support the conclusion that Spanish does not hinder academic achievement as stated in 5.4 above, rather, the findings provide evidence that exposure to Spanish in a school environment may serve to promote the academic achievement of certain populations. Moreover, a desire to engage in higher level scholarly activities with Spanish is reflected in 25% of the College Student informants who are pursing the field as a major.

5.6 LIMITATIONS OF THE STUDY

Accompanying the above results and conclusions is the acknowledgement of certain limitations of the study. First, while self-reported proficiency has long been utilized in sociolinguistic research, the reliability of such a subjective measure can be questioned. In an attempt to provide a more quantitative measure of proficiency, a vocabulary test was employed for the High School Student and College Student informants. The results of this technique demonstrated that informants largely underestimated their own proficiency in Spanish, but it is not known how generally reliable the measure is either. Thus, more reliable means of assessing bilingual proficiency must be developed.

Additional concerns can be raised regarding the sample selection. High School Dropout informants were solicited largely through word of mouth and by targeting social service agencies where high concentrations of Mexican youths were expected to be found. Additionally, for unknown reasons and with efforts made to the contrary, the High School Student sample was imbalanced with regard to gender, with males greatly outnumbering females. Still, the large pool of High School Student informants diminishes the bias in this imbalance. Lastly, some College Student informants who participated in the present study were informed by announcements made in Spanish classes. As a result 25% of the College Student informants could have been positively biased toward Spanish since they claimed Spanish as one of their majors. Still, in light of the high degree of consistency in the College Student informants' responses, this characteristic was not felt to diminish the effects of the overall conclusions. Nonetheless, with respect to the College Student informants, caution must be exercised in interpreting these results beyond the population that was examined here.

The manner in which the survey was administrated may have also influenced the results. High School Dropout informants, in order to control for level of literacy, were orally interviewed. Due to both time constraints as well as the great number of individuals interviewed, High School Student informants were allowed to fill out the survey individually while the researcher monitored their progress and provided clarification. College Student informants, by virtue of their academic status, were not envisioned as having a literacy impairment and thus were allowed to freely fill out the survey with guidance by the researcher when necessary as in the case of the High School Student informants. As a consequence of a lesser researcher-controlled administration of the instrument, High School Student and College Student inadvertently skipped over items.[2]

The location in which the interviews took place may have influenced the results. Both High School Dropout and High School Student informants were interviewed in the Chicago area, in their native, bilingual environment. College Student informants, on the other hand, were interviewed some 150 miles south, on the campus of the University of Illinois, where the linguistic constraints favor the use of English to an almost exclusive degree. Had the College Student informants also been interviewed in the Chicago area, it is anticipated that their interpersonal communication would have been weighted more toward Spanish.

5.7 AREAS FOR FUTURE RESEARCH

While the present study has provided some insight regarding the impact of Spanish on academic achievement of Mexican youths and the sociolinguistic characteristics of the Mexican community in the Midwest, this research has questioned the relevance of the findings of previous dropout and sociolinguistic endeavors and thus opened new avenues of inquiry that need to be explored. First, Latino dropouts have often been measured in terms of standards that are not culturally relevant, despite the fact that several measures that have traditionally been used as indicators of dropouts were found to be irrelevant to this population. An effort needs to be made within the research community to identify those factors that are more appropriate predictors of school leaving among Latino (e.g. Valdivieso 1986), and in particular, Mexican communities (e.g. Valverde 1986). Moreover, simply identifying the symptoms of Latino dropout is not enough; further investigation is also needed to identify the factors that contribute to Latino academic success. Since it has been established that informants here looked to their siblings as role models, one area clearly in need of further examination is that of first generation college students, that is, those individuals who are the first in their family to attend college.

Just as we cannot be satisfied with pointing out the shortcomings of Latino dropouts, the factors that have been found to be positively associated with academic achievement such as bilingual education and Spanish-only education (and perhaps courses in Spanish language, history and culture) must be viewed with caution. Further research needs to be undertaken to more identify both the objectives and practices of these programs in order to more fully understand their academic and sociolinguistic impact. Moreover, the present study has revealed the need of more valid, reliable and practical means of assessing bilingual proficiency in adults. Given the potential that bilingual education has for enhancing the academic achievement of Spanish-speaking youths, it is important that we be able to accurately assess the benefits obtained through exposure to such programs.

Additionally, the Midwest Mexican informants in the present study displayed language choice and language attitudes patterns that diverged from those of Southwest informants. These findings indicate that language use and language attitude patterns are different in different regions. Furthermore, the lack of studies exploring the sociolinguistic traits of Midwest Spanish-speakers reveal that endeavors have failed to fully examine the regional differences that exist among groups of the same national origin. These findings point to the need of more current efforts to document the use and attitudes of Spanish-speaking populations and emphasize the need to expand those efforts to include a wider variety of geographic areas.

Finally, the impact that the rapidly expanding U.S. Latino population currently has and will continue to have on this country's demography and economy is clearly evident. This influence, coupled with the high school dropout rate among Latinos that currently stands at epidemic proportions, stress both the need and the urgency with which these research issues must be addressed.

NOTES

1. Many informants in all three groups selected the option of "Undecided" for this statement.

2. For example, some details about interlocutor characteristics were left blank by these groups.

Appendix of Research Materials

High School Dropout Questionnaire—English

University of Illinois
at Urbana-Champaign

Department of Spanish,
Italian, and Portuguese
4080 Foreign Languages Building   217 333-3390
707 South Mathews Avenue   217 244-0190 *fax*
Urbana, IL 61801   *E-mail:* sip@uiuc.edu
                                Urbana, June 1993

Dear prospective participant:

As it has been mentioned to you by our interviewer, we are conducting a study on Latino/a students who have dropped out of school. This study is being conducted at the Department of Spanish, Italian and Portuguese at the University of Illinois at Urbana-Champaign. The purpose of our study is to find out what are the reasons for dropping out and the issues which should be addressed in hopes to lower the dropout rate among Latino students.

Your participation is **VOLUNTARY** and strictly **ANONYMOUS**. If you agree to participate, the interviewer will read to you some questions (you can look at the questions with her if you wish) and she will write down your answers. You are free not to answer questions you might feel offend you.
The interview will take between 20 and 30 minutes.

We thank you for your interest in our study. Be assured that the results will be used to help the Latino community.

                                                    Urbana, junio de 1993
Estimado futuro participante:

Como ya le ha mencionado nuestra entrevistadora, estamos haciendo un estudio sobre aquellos estudiantes latinos que han dejado la escuela secundaria. Este estudio se está llevando a cabo en el Departamento de Español, Italiano y Portugués de la Universidad de Illinois en Urbana-Champaign. El propósito de nuestro estudio es ver cuáles son los las razones que impulsan a los estudiantes latinos a dejar la escuela y, ver cuáles son los aspectos en los que se debe poner atención para bajar el número de estudiantes latinos que dejan la escuela.

Su participación en este estudio es **VOLUNTARIA** y **ANONIMA**. Si acepta participar, la entrevistadora le leerá unas preguntas (que usted puede mirar también si desea) y escribirá sus respuestas. Usted tiene la libertad de no responder aquellas preguntas que le parezcan ofensivas. La entrevista toma entre 20 y 30 minutos.

Le agradecemos por su interés en nuestro estudio. Esté seguro/a que los resultados serán utilizados para ayudar a la comunidad latina.

Answer Guide

Please use the appropriate section as stated on the questionnaire.

A.   Spanish   English   Both

B.   Excellent   Well   Fair   Poor

C.   Language used:

1. Spanish only
2. Mostly Spanish, but with some English
3. English and Spanish equally
4. Mostly English, but with some Spanish
5. English only

D.   Topics of Conversation:
  - Politics
  - Religion
  - School
  - Medical issues
  - Family issues
  - Childhood or past
  - Dreams and thoughts
  - Other _____

E.   Typical Grades
  - Mostly A's
  - A's and B's
  - Mostly B's
  - B's and C's
  - Mostly C's
  - C's and D's
  - Mostly D's
  - D's and F's
  - Mostly F's

F.   Never/Very Rarely   Sometimes   Very Often/Always

G.   Very Important   Somewhat Important   Not Important

H.   Very Likely   Possible   Very Unlikely

I.   Agree   Disagree   Undecided

No _____

1. Age_____   2. Sex: M   F   3. Place of birth_____ , _____.
                                                   state   country
              If not born in the United States, how old were you when you came? _____

4. Last grade you completed _____   5. Year you dropped out _____
6. Why did you drop out of high school? _____
7. Name two negative factors which you couldn't overcome to finish high school
_____   _____
8. Who did you discuss your decision to drop out with?_____
9. Did your best friend in high school agree with this decision?   Y   N
10. Have you considered returning for your high school diploma or GED?   Y   N

11. Are you currently employed? Y   N

12. When you refer to yourself ethnically or culturally, you say that you are_____
(Please use any term or terms you use.)

13. Please answer the following questions using section A or B from the answer sheet.

    a. You first learned to **speak** (A.)_____
    b. You first learned to **read** (A.)_____
    c. You first learned to **write** (A.)_____

    d. You feel that You **speak** Spanish (B.)_____
    e. You feel that You **understand** Spanish (B.)_____
    f. You feel that You can **read** Spanish (B.)_____
    g. You feel that You can **write** Spanish (B.)_____
    h. You feel that You **speak** English (B.) _____
    i. You feel that You **understand** English (B.)_____
    j. You feel that You can **read** English (B.)_____
    k. You feel that You can **write** English (B.)_____

14. Please fill in the following chart about your family members with whom you speak frequently.
Please mention
    if they are male or female relatives and use sections C and D from the answer sheet where shown.

	Age	Born in	This person	You speak to this	You typically speak to this
	(roughly)	(country)	speaks... (C.)	person at home in... (C.)	person about... (D.)
Parents					
Mother	_____	_____	_____	_____	P R S M F C D O_
Father	_____	_____	_____	_____	P R S M F C D O_
Brothers/Sisters					
M F	_____	_____	_____	_____	P R S M F C D O_
M F	_____	_____	_____	_____	P R S M F C D O_
M F	_____	_____	_____	_____	P R S M F C D O_
M F	_____	_____	_____	_____	P R S M F C D O_
M F	_____	_____	_____	_____	P R S M F C D O_
M F	_____	_____	_____	_____	P R S M F C D O_
M F	_____	_____	_____	_____	P R S M F C D O_
M F	_____	_____	_____	_____	P R S M F C D O_
M F	_____	_____	_____	_____	P R S M F C D O_

M F					P R S M F C D O_
Cousins					
M F	____	____	____	____	P R S M F C D O_
M F	____	____	____	____	P R S M F C D O_
M F	____	____	____	____	P R S M F C D O_
M F	____	____	____	____	P R S M F C D O_
M F	____	____	____	____	P R S M F C D O_
M F	____	____	____	____	P R S M F C D O_
Aunts/Uncles					
M F	____	____	____	____	P R S M F C D O_
M F	____	____	____	____	P R S M F C D O_
M F	____	____	____	____	P R S M F C D O_
M F	____	____	____	____	P R S M F C D O_
M F	____	____	____	____	P R S M F C D O_
Nieces/Nephews					
M F	____	____	____	____	P R S M F C D O_
M F	____	____	____	____	P R S M F C D O_
M F	____	____	____	____	P R S M F C D O_
M F	____	____	____	____	P R S M F C D O_
M F	____	____	____	____	P R S M F C D O_
Grandparents					
M F	____	____	____	____	P R S M F C D O_
M F	____	____	____	____	P R S M F C D O_
M F	____	____	____	____	P R S M F C D O_
M F	____	____	____	____	P R S M F C D O_
Best Friend					
M F	____	____	____	____	P R S M F C D O_
M F	____	____	____	____	P R S M F C D O_

15. a. Mother's occupation:_____ b. Last grade she completed _____

16. a. Father's occupation:_____ b. Last grade he completed _____

17. At your permanent address, who is the head of your house?_____

18. How many brothers and sisters do you have that
    a. finished high school and continued studying?   ____
    b. finished high school and started working?   ____
    c. dropped out of high school and did or is doing the GED?   ____
    d. dropped out of high school and has not done the GED?   ____
    e. are older and never went to high school?   ____
    f. are now in school?   ____
    g. are too young to go to school?   ____

19. Have you ever taken a class (other than a language class) where the teacher taught only in Spanish?
    Y N
        If yes, what grade levels?_____ Where was/were the school(s)?_____

20. Were you ever in a bilingual education program?   Y N
        If yes, what grade levels?_____ Where was/were the school(s)?_____

21. Did you ever repeat a grade? Y N   How many times? _____

22. Please answer the following questions about your **high school experiences** the best that you can.

    a. How would you describe your course work at high school?: (Please check one)
        ____college preparatory (advanced courses in math, science, rhetoric, literature, history)
        ____general (basic courses in math or science, creative writing, etc.)
        ____vocational (remedial or basic courses in math/English, home economics, shop, work
          -study)

    b. What grades did you usually get ? (Use Section E from the answer sheet) _____

    c. Did you ever cut class? Y N
    d. Were you ever suspended or put on probation? Y N
    e. Were you ever in serious trouble with the law? Y N
    f. Did you ever participate in any extracurricular activities offered by your school (sports, clubs)? Y
    g. Were you popular in school? Y N
    h. Did you have a positive attitude about yourself? Y N
    i. Did you feel that you were able to do things as well as most other people? Y N
    j. Did you feel that good luck was more important than hard work? Y N
    k. Did you feel that others were stopping you from getting ahead? Y N

23. When you were in high school, how much did your parents...

    a. ...speak with teachers or other school officials? (F) _____
    b. ...help you with your homework? (F) _____
    c. ...talk about your plans after finishing high school? (F) _____
    d. ...take you to museums or other cultural events? (F) _____
    e. ...know exactly where you were during non-school hours? (F) _____

24. Answer the following questions about your best friend during high school

    a. Did he/she ever cut class? Y N
    b. Was he/she ever suspended or put on probation? Y N
    c. Was he/she ever in serious trouble with the law? Y N
    d. Did he/she ever participate in any extracurricular activities offered
       by your school (sports, clubs)? Y N
    e. Was he/she popular in school? Y N
    f. Is he/she still your best friend now? Y N
    g. Did he/she finish high school? Y N

    h. What sex is your best friend? _____
    i. What is your best friend doing now? _____

25. When you were in high school, how important was the following to you?

    a. finding a steady job (G) _____
    b. having close friends (G) _____
    c. Having lots of money (G) _____
    d. Living close to parents (G) _____
    e. Moving away from the area in which you lived (G) _____

26. When you were in high school, how much of your free time did you spend

    a. studying and doing homework? (F) _____
    b. hanging out with friends? (F) _____
    c. thinking and daydreaming alone? (F) _____

    d. reading for pleasure? (F) _____
    e. with your family ? (F) _____

27. Did you have a job when you were in high school? Y N
    If yes,
        a. ...did you find your job more enjoyable than school? Y N
        b. ...did you feel your job was more important than school? Y N

        c. ... please fill in the following information

During what grades?	For how long?	How many hours per week?	Did you speak Spanish regularly to your... boss?	coworkers?	customers?
_____	_____ _____	Y N	Y N	Y N
_____	_____ _____	Y N	Y N	Y N
_____	_____ _____	Y N	Y N	Y N

28. When you have equal access to English and Spanish television, radio and print media...
    a. you most often watch TV shows in (C.) _____
    b. you most often watch the news in (C.) _____
    c. you most often listen to the radio or music in (C.) _____
    d. you most often read the newspaper in (C.) _____
    e. you most often read magazines in (C.) _____
    f. you most often read books in (C.) _____

29. a. When you add up numbers in your head you do it in (C.) _____
    b. When you are alone, your thoughts are in (C.) _____
    c. When you are alone, your prayers are in (C.) _____
    d. Your dreams are in (C.)_____

30. When the person you're speaking to is bilingual...

    a. ...and you're happy you can best express yourself in (C.) _____
    b. ...and you're mad you can best express yourself in (C.) _____
    c. ...and you're nervous you can best express yourself in (C.) _____
    d. ...and you're sad you can best express yourself in (C.)_____
    e. ...and you're trying to win an argument , you speak in (C.)_____
    f. ...and you're asking for general information, you speak in (C.)_____
    g. ...and you're explaining how something mechanical works, you speak in (C.)_____
    h. ...and you're ordering them to do something, you speak in (C.)_____
    i. ...and you talk about home events you usually speak in (C.)_____
    j. ...and you gossip about someone, you usually speak in (C.)_____
    k. ...and you talk about school events, you usually speak in (C.)_____
    l. ...and you talk about work events, you usually speak in (C.)_____
    m. ...and you talk about world events, you usually speak in (C.)_____

31. How likely are you to become <u>close</u> friends with:
    a. Latinos who speak only Spanish (H.) _____
    b. Latinos who speak only English (H.) _____
    c. Latinos who are bilingual (H.) _____
    d. Non-Latinos who speak only English (H.) _____
    e. Non-Latinos who are Spanish/English bilinguals (H.) _____

32. The following statements refer to Spanish. Please say if you Agree, Disagree or are Undecided.

    a. You prefer to speak Spanish rather than English. (I.) _____
    b. You feel proud that you speak Spanish (I.) _____
    c. You feel lucky that you speak Spanish. (I.) _____
    d. It is important to you to be able to speak Spanish. (I.) _____
    e. A person can have more job opportunities if they know Spanish. (I.) _____
    f. You can communicate with more people by speaking Spanish. (I.) _____
    g. Spanish is a useful language to know. (I.) _____
    h. Knowing Spanish helps you seem more educated to others. (I.) _____
    i. You feel more comfortable around people who speak Spanish. (I.) _____
    j. Spanish helps you make friends. (I.) _____
    k. Speaking Spanish makes you feel like you belong to a group. (I.) _____
    l. Speaking Spanish is an important part of your family life. (I.) _____
    m. Speaking Spanish is an important part of your school life. (I.) _____
    n. Speaking Spanish is an important part of your social life. (I.) _____
    o. You feel closer to friends who speak Spanish. (I.) _____
    p. Bilingual education programs should develop Spanish skills for all students. (I.) _____
    q. Bilingual education programs should develop Spanish skills for Latino students. (I.) _____
    r. Latinos should know Spanish. (I.) _____
    s. Spanish is an essential part of your culture. (I.) _____
    t. When you have children, you want them to be able to speak Spanish. (I.) _____
    u. Spanish helps your community progress. (I.) _____

33. The following questions refer to English. Please say if you Agree, Disagree or are Undecided.

    a. You prefer to speak English than Spanish. (I.) _____
    b. You feel proud that you speak English (I.) _____
    c. You feel lucky that you speak English. (I.) _____
    d. It is important to you to be able to speak English. (I.) _____
    e. A person can have more job opportunities if they know English. (I.) _____
    f. You can communicate with more people by speaking English. (I.) _____
    g. English is a useful language to know. (I.) _____
    h. Knowing English helps you seem more educated to others. (I.) _____
    i. You feel more comfortable around people who speak English. (I.) _____
    j. English helps you make friends. (I.) _____
    k. Speaking English makes you feel like you belong to a group. (I.) _____
    l. Speaking English is an important part of your family life. (I.) _____
    m. Speaking English is an important part of your school life. (I.) _____
    n. Speaking English is an important part of your social life. (I.) _____
    o. You feel closer to your friends who speak English. (I.) _____
    p. Bilingual education programs should develop English skills for Latino students. (I.) _____
    q. Latinos should know English. (I.) _____
    r. English is a threat to your culture. (I.) _____
    s. English helps your community progress. (I.) _____

34. Please say which language or languages is/are most appropriate for the following situations. (refer to A)

  a. Science (A.)_____
  b. Military commands (A.)_____
  c. Religious rituals (A.)_____
  d. Politics (A.)_____
  e. Novels (A.)_____
  f. Poetry (A.)_____
  g. Folksongs (A.)_____
  h. Bargaining (A.)_____
  i. Joking (A.)_____
  j. Cursing (A.)_____
  k. Speaking to babies (A.)_____
  l. Lying (A.)_____
  m. Persuading (A.)_____

35. For each pair of characteristics, please circle the number on the scale that represents how you feel about the **Spanish** language.

Beautiful	1	2	3	4	5	Ugly
Rich	1	2	3	4	5	Poor
Noisy	1	2	3	4	5	Musical
Precise	1	2	3	4	5	Vague
Illogical	1	2	3	4	5	Logical
Simple	1	2	3	4	5	Sophisticated
Rhythmical	1	2	3	4	5	Irregular
Refined	1	2	3	4	5	Vulgar
Bland	1	2	3	4	5	Colorful
Intimate	1	2	3	4	5	Public
Superior	1	2	3	4	5	Inferior
Impure	1	2	3	4	5	Pure
Soothing	1	2	3	4	5	Unnerving
Graceful	1	2	3	4	5	Clumsy
Profane	1	2	3	4	5	Sacred

High School Dropout Questionnaire—Spanish

University of Illinois   Department of Spanish,
at Urbana-Champaign   Italian, and Portuguese

4080 Foreign Languages Building   217 333-3390
707 South Mathews Avenue   217 244-0190 *fax*
Urbana, IL 61801   *E-mail:* sip@uiuc.edu

Urbana, June 1993

Dear prospective participant:

As it has been mentioned to you by our interviewer, we are conducting a
study on Latino/a students who have dropped out of school. This study is
being conducted at the Department of Spanish, Italian and Portuguese at the University of
Illinois at Urbana-Champaign. The purpose of our study is to
find out what are the reasons for dropping out and the issues which should
be addressed in hopes to lower the dropout rate among Latino students.

Your participation is **VOLUNTARY** and strictly **ANONYMOUS.** If you agree
to participate, the interviewer will read to you some questions (you can
look at the questions with her if you wish) and she will write down your answers. You are free
not to answer questions you might feel offend you.
The interview will take between 20 and 30 minutes.

We thank you for your interest in our study. Be assured that the results will
be used to help the Latino community.

Urbana, junio de 1993

Estimado futuro participante:

Como ya le ha mencionado nuestra entrevistadora, estamos haciendo un
estudio sobre aquellos estudiantes latinos que han dejado la escuela
secundaria. Este estudio se está llevando a cabo en el Departamento de
Español, Italiano y Portugués de la Universidad de Illinois en Urbana-
Champaign. El propósito de nuestro estudio es ver cuáles son los las razones que impulsan a
los estudiantes latinos a dejar la escuela y, ver cuáles son
los aspectos en los que se debe poner atención para bajar el número de estudiantes latinos
que dejan la escuela.

Su participación en este estudio es **VOLUNTARIA** y **ANONIMA.** Si acepta participar, la
entrevistadora le leerá unas preguntas (que usted puede mirar también si desea) y escribirá sus
respuestas. Usted tiene la libertad de no responder aquellas preguntas que le parezcan
ofensivas. La entrevista toma entre 20 y 30 minutos.

Le agradecemos por su interés en nuestro estudio. Esté seguro/a que los resultados serán
utilizados para ayudar a la comunidad latina.

Hoja de Respuestas

Favor de usar la sección apropiada según se indique en el cuestionario.

A.   Español   Inglés   Ambos

B.   Excelente   Muy Bien   Regular Mal

C.   Idioma que se usa:

    1. Solamente español
    2. Mayormente español, pero mezclado con inglés
    3. Inglés y español igual
    4. Mayormente inglés, pero mezclado con español
    5. Solamente inglés

D.   Temas de Conversación:
    la Política
    la Religión
    la eScuela
    Asuntos Medicos
    Asuntos Familiares
    Cuando era niño o el pasado
    Deseos y pensamientos
    Otro_____

E.   Mayormente A's
    A's y B's
    Mayormente B's
    B's y C's
    Mayormente C's
    C's y D's
    Mayormente D's
    D's y F's
    Mayormente F's

F.   Nunca/Rara Vez   A Veces   A Menudo

G.   Muy Importante   Algo Importante   No Importante

H.   Muy Probable   Possible   No Muy Probable

I.   De Acuerdo   No De Acuerdo Indeciso

No _____

1. Edad_____   2. Sexo: M   F   3. Lugar de nacimiento_____ , _____ .
                                                   estado   país
                Si no nació en los EEUU, ¿cuántos años tenía cuando vino? _____

4. Ultimo grado que terminó   1   2   3   4   5. Año en que se salió: 19_____

6. ¿Cuál fue la razón principal de por qué se salió de la escuela? _____
7. ¿Qué otros factores influyeron en su decisión? _____   _____
8. ¿Con quién(es) habló Ud. sobre su decisión de salirse de la escuela?_____
9. ¿Estuvo de acuerdo su mejor amigo con esta decisión?   Sí   No   No sé
10. ¿Ha pensado en regresar a la escuela para sacar el diploma o el GED?   Sí   No

11. ¿Tiene trabajo ahora?   Sí   No

12. Cuando Ud. se refiere a sí mismo de manera étnica o cultural, Ud. dice que es _____
      (Favor de mencionar el (los) término(s) que Ud. utiliza.)

13. Favor de contestar las preguntas a continuación utilizando las secciones A o B (según se indique)
de la hoja de respuestas.

        a. Ud. primero aprendió a **hablar** (A.)_____
        b. Ud. primero aprendió a **leer** (A.)_____
        c. Ud. primero aprendió a **escribir** (A.)_____

        d. Ud. cree que **habla** español (B.)_____
        e. Ud. cree que **entiende** español (B.)_____
        f. Ud. cree que puede **leer** español (B.)_____
        g. Ud. cree que puede **escribir** español (B.)_____
        h. Ud. cree que **habla** inglés (B.) _____
        i. Ud. cree que **entiende** inglés (B.)_____
        j. Ud. cree que puede **leer** Inglés (B.)_____
        k. Ud. cree que puede **escribir** Inglés (B.)_____

14. Rellene la tabla que aparece abajo sobre los familia res y amigos <u>con quienes habla con frecuencia</u>
Mencione si la persona es masculina o femenina y utilice las secciones C y D de la hoja de respuestas
según se indique.

	Edad	Nació en	Esta persona	En casa Ud. le	Tipicamente, Ud. habla con
	(aproximada)	(país)	habla... (C.)	habla en...(C.)	esta persona sobre...(D.)
Padres					
Madre	_____	_____	_____	_____	P R S M F C D O____
Padre	_____	_____	_____	_____	P R S M F C D O____
Hermanos					
M F	_____	_____	_____	_____	P R S M F C D O____
M F	_____	_____	_____	_____	P R S M F C D O____
M F	_____	_____	_____	_____	P R S M F C D O____
M F	_____	_____	_____	_____	P R S M F C D O____
M F	_____	_____	_____	_____	P R S M F C D O____
M F	_____	_____	_____	_____	P R S M F C D O____
Primos					
M F	_____	_____	_____	_____	P R S M F C D O____
M F	_____	_____	_____	_____	P R S M F C D O____
M F	_____	_____	_____	_____	P R S M F C D O____
M F	_____	_____	_____	_____	P R S M F C D O____

Tíos
M F	___	___	___	___	P R S M F C D O ___
M F	___	___	___	___	P R S M F C D O ___
M F	___	___	___	___	P R S M F C D O ___
M F	___	___	___	___	P R S M F C D O ___

Sobrinos
M F	___	___	___	___	P R S M F C D O ___
M F	___	___	___	___	P R S M F C D O ___
M F	___	___	___	___	P R S M F C D O ___

Abuelos
| M F | ___ | ___ | ___ | ___ | P R S M F C D O ___ |
| M F | ___ | ___ | ___ | ___ | P R S M F C D O ___ |

Mejores Amigos
| M F | ___ | ___ | ___ | ___ | P R S M F C D O ___ |
| M F | ___ | ___ | ___ | ___ | P R S M F C D O ___ |

15. a. Ocupación de su madre: _____   b. Ultimo grado que ella terminó _____

16. a. Ocupación de su padre: _____   b. Ultimo grado que él terminó _____

17. En su domicilio permanente, ¿quién se encarga de la casa? _____

18. ¿Cuántos hermanos/as tiene Ud. que

      a. terminaron la escuela y siguieron estudiando? _____
      b. terminaron la escuela y empezaron a trabajar? _____
      c. abandonaron la escuela y sacaron o están sacando el GED? _____
      d. abandonaron la escuela y no sacaron ni están sacando el GED? _____
      e. son adultos y nunca fueron a la escuela? _____
      f. asisten todavía a escuelas primarias o secundarias? _____
      g. son todavía demasiado pequeños para asistir a la escuela? _____

19. ¿Participó Ud. alguna vez en un programa bilingüe?   Sí No
    Si responde que sí, ¿en qué grado(s)? _____ ¿Dónde fue(ron) la(s) escuela(s)? _____

20. ¿Ha estado alguna vez en un curso (que no sea de idiomas) en donde el maestro sólo enseñaba en español? Sí No   Si responde que sí, ¿en qué grado(s)? _____ ¿Dónde fue(ron) la(s) escuela(s)? _____

21. ¿Repitió alguna vez un grado?   Sí   No   ¿Cuántas veces? _____

22. Conteste las siguientes preguntas sobre sus **experiencias en la escuela secundaria** lo mejor que pueda.

    a. ¿Cómo describiría sus cursos en la secundaria?: (Marcar uno)
        ___ preparatorios para la universidad (cursos avanzados de matemáticas, ciencias; retórica, literatura)
        ___ generales (cursos básicos de matemáticas, ciencias; composición básica)
        ___ vocacionales (cursos básicos/remediales de matemáticas, inglés, estudios domésticos, talleres)

    b. ¿Qué calificaciones sacaba Ud.? (Mire la sección E de la hoja de respuestas) _____

    c. ¿Alguna vez se fue de pinta (faltó a clases voluntariamente)?   (Mire la sección F)

d. ¿Alguna vez fue suspendido o puesto en período de prueba?　　Sí　No
e. ¿Alguna vez tuvo problemas serios con la policía?　　Sí　No
f. ¿Alguna vez participó en actividades extracurriculares ofrecidas por la escuela (deportes/ clubs)?　Sí　No
g. ¿Era Ud. popular?　　Sí　No
h. ¿Tenía Ud. una actitud positiva hacia sí mismo? Sí　No
i. ¿Se sentía con igual capacidad que cualquier otra persona?　　Sí　No
j. ¿Sentía que la buena suerte era más importante que el trabajo? Sí　No
k. ¿Sentía que otros le impedían progresar?　　Sí　No

23. Mirando la sección F, cuando Ud. asistía a la escuela secundaria, sus padres...

    a. ...¿cuánto hablaban con los maestros y otros oficiales de la escuela?　(F) _____
    b. ...¿cuánto le ayudaban con su tarea?　(F) _____
    c. ...¿cuánto le hablaban de sus planes de cuando terminara la escuela?　(F) _____
    d. ...¿cuánto le llevaban a museos o funciones culturales?　(F) _____
    e. ...¿cuánto sabían exactamente dónde encontrarlo(la) después de clases?　(F) _____

24. Conteste las siguientes preguntas sobre su mejor amigo/a en la escuela secundaria.
    a. ¿Alguna vez se fue de pinta (faltó a clases voluntariamente)?　(Mire la sección F)
    b. ¿Alguna vez fue suspendido o puesto en período de prueba?　Sí　No
    c. ¿Alguna vez tuvo problemas serios con la policía?　　Sí　No
    d. ¿Alguna vez participó en actividades extracurriculares ofrecidas por la escuela (deportes/ clubs)?　Sí　No
    e. ¿Era él (ella) popular?　　Sí　No
    f. ¿Sigue siendo su mejor amigo/a?　Sí　No
    g. ¿Terminó él (ella) la secundaria?　Sí　No
    h. ¿Es su mejor amigo hombre o mujer?　_____
    i. ¿Qué hace él (ella) ahora?　_____

25. Cuando Ud. asistía a la secundaria, ¿qué tan importante era lo siguiente?　(Mire sección G)
    a. encontrar un trabajo fijo　(G) _____
    b. tener buenos amigos (G) _____
    c. tener mucho dinero(G) _____
    d. vivir cerca de sus padres (G) _____
    e. mudarse a otro barrio　(G) _____

26. Cuando Ud. asistía a la secundaria, ¿cómo pasaba su tiempo libre ?　(Mire sección F)
    a. estudiando y haciendo la tarea?　(F) _____
    b. con sus amigos?　(F) _____
    c. a solas pensando y soñando?　(F) _____
    d. leyendo por placer?　(F) _____
    e. con su familia?　(F) _____

27. Tenía trabajo mientras asistía a la secundaria?   Sí   No
    Si responde que sí,
    a. ...encontró que trabajar era más divertido que ir a la escuela?   Sí   No
    b. ...sintió que trabajar era más importante que ir a la escuela?   Sí   No
    c. ... favor de rellenar la información abajo.

¿Durante qué grados trabajó?	¿Por cuánto tiempo?	¿Cuántas horas por semana?	Hablaba español regularmente con...		
			... el jefe?	...sus compañeros?	...los clientes?
————	———— ———	Sí No	Sí No	Sí No
————	———— ———	Sí No	Sí No	Sí No
————	———— ———	Sí No	Sí No	Sí No

28. Mirando la sección C, ¿qué lengua usa más frecuentemente cuando...
    a. mira las noticias en la televisión   (C.) ____
    b. mira otros programas de televisión   (C.) ____
    c. escucha la radio o música (C.) ____
    d. lee el periódico más (C.) ____
    e. lee revistas más   (C.) ____
    f. lee libros más (C.) ____

29. Mirando la sección C, ¿qué lengua usa cuando...

    a. ...suma números mentalmente? (C.) ____
    b. ...está solo y piensa? (C.) ____
    c. ...está solo y reza? (C.) ____
    d. ...sueña ? (C.)____

30. Mirando la sección C, ¿qué lengua usa cuando la persona con quien está hablando es bilingüe y...

    a. ...Ud. está contento? (C.) ____
    b. ...Ud. está enojado? (C.) ____
    c. ...Ud. está nervioso? (C.) ____
    d. ...Ud. está triste? (C.)____
    e. ...Ud. está tratando de ganar la discusión? (C.)____
    f. ...Ud. está explicando cómo funciona algo mecánico? (C.)____
    g. ...Ud. le está ordenando hacer algo? (C.)____
    h. ...Ud. habla de temas familiares? (C.)____
    i. ...Ud. chismea de alguien? (C.)____
    j. ...Ud. habla de cosas del trabajo? (C.)____
    k. ...Ud. habla de eventos mundiales? (C.)____

31. Mirando la sección H, ¿qué tan probable es que Ud. se haga amigo íntimo de
    a. Latinos que solamente hablan español? (H.) ____
    b. Latinos que solamente hablan inglés? (H.) ____
    c. Latinos que son bilingües? (H.) ____
    d. No-Latinos que solamente hablan inglés? (H.) ____
    e. No-Latinos que son bilingües? (H.) ____

32. Las siguientes oraciones se refieren al **español**, responda según las opciones de la sección I.

    a. Ud. prefiere hablar español más que inglés. (I.) ____
    b. Ud. se siente orgulloso de hablar español   (I.) ____
    c. Ud. se siente afortunado de hablar español. (I.) ____
    d. Es importante para Ud. poder hablar español . (I.) ____

e. Uno tiene más oportunidades de empleo si sabe español. (I.) _____
f. Uno puede comunicarse con más gente si sabe español. (I.) _____
g. El español es un idioma útil. (I.) _____
h. El saber español hace que otros lo vean como más culto (educado). (I.) _____
i. Se siente más cómodo con gente que habla español. (I.) _____
j. El español le ayuda a hacer amigos. (I.) _____
k. El hablar español le hace sentirseque forma parte de un grupo. (I.) _____
l. El hablar español es importante para su vida familiar. (I.) _____
m. El hablar español fue importante para su vida escolar. (I.) _____
n. El hablar español es importante para su vida social. (I.) _____
o. La educación bilingüe debe ayudar a todos a desarrollar sus habilidades en español. (I.) _____
p. La educación bilingüe debe ayudar a los latinos a desarrollar sus habilidades
   en español. (I.) _____
q. Los latinos deben saber español. (I.) _____
r. El español es una parte importante de la cultura latina. (I.) _____
s. Cuando tenga hijos, Ud. quiere que aprendan español. (I.) _____
t. El español ayuda a nuestra comunidad a progresar. (I.) _____

33. Las siguientes oraciones se refieren al **inglés**, responda según las opciones de la sección I.

a. Ud. prefiere hablar inglés más que español. (I.) _____
b. Ud. se siente orgulloso de hablar inglés (I.) _____
c. Ud. se siente afortunado de hablar inglés. (I.) _____
d. Es importante para Ud. poder hablar inglés. (I.) _____
e. Uno tiene más oportunidades de empleo si sabe inglés. (I.) _____
f. Uno puede comunicarse con más gente si sabe inglés. (I.) _____
g. El inglés es un idioma útil. (I.) _____
h. El saber inglés hace que otros lo vean como más culto (educado). (I.) _____
i. Se siente más cómodo con gente que habla inglés. (I.) _____
j. El inglés le ayuda a hacer amigos. (I.) _____
k. El hablar inglés le hace sentirse que forma parte de un grupo. (I.) _____
l. El hablar inglés es importante para su vida familiar. (I.) _____
m. El hablar inglés fue importante para su vida escolar. (I.) _____
n. El hablar inglés es importante para su vida social. (I.) _____
o. La educación bilingüe debe ayudar a los latinos a desarrollar habilidades en inglés. (I.) _____
p. Los latinos deben saber inglés. (I.) _____
q. El inglés es una amenaza a la cultura latina. (I.) _____
r. El inglés ayuda a nuestra comunidad a progresar. (I.) _____

34. Según las opciones de la sección A, mencione qué idioma(s) cree Ud. que es (son) más
apropiado(s) para los siguientes temas.

a. la ciencia (A.)_____
b. las órdenes militares (A.)_____
c. los ritos religiosos (A.)_____
d. la política (A.)_____
e. las novelas (A.)_____
f. la poesía (A.)_____
g. los cantos folklóricos (A.)_____
h. el regateo (A.)_____
i. las bromas (A.)_____
j. las maldiciones (A.)_____
k. el hablar con niños (A.)_____
l. el mentir (A.)_____
m. el persuadir (A.)_____

35. Para cada par de características, señale el número en la escala que representa cómo Ud. se siente hacia el **español**.

Bonito	1	2	3	4	5	Feo
Rico	1	2	3	4	5	Pobre
Ruidoso	1	2	3	4	5	Musical
Preciso	1	2	3	4	5	Vago
Ilógico	1	2	3	4	5	Lógico
Sencillo	1	2	3	4	5	Sofisticado
Rítmico	1	2	3	4	5	Irregular
Refinado	1	2	3	4	5	Vulgar
Sin color	1	2	3	4	5	Colorido
Privado	1	2	3	4	5	Público
Superior	1	2	3	4	5	Inferior
No puro	1	2	3	4	5	Puro
Tranquilo	1	2	3	4	5	Nervioso
Agil	1	2	3	4	5	Torpe
Común	1	2	3	4	5	Sagrado

High School Student Questionnaire—English

Instructor _____   No. _____

Urbana, January 1995

Dear Student:

As has been mentioned to you by the researcher, we are conducting a study on Latino/a students. This study is being conducted at the Department of Spanish, Italian and Portuguese at the University of Illinois at Urbana-Champaign. The purpose of our study is to explore the language characteristics of bilingual youths at different academic levels.

Your participation is **VOLUNTARY** and strictly **ANONYMOUS**. If you agree to participate, the researcher will guide you through the survey and instruct you on how to mark your answers. You are free not to answer questions you might feel offend you. The interview will take no more than 45 minutes to complete.

Thank you for your interest in our study.

Answer Guide

A. Language used:

1. Spanish only
2. Mostly Spanish, but mixed with some English
3. Sometimes only Spanish, sometimes only English
4. Mostly English, but mixed with some Spanish
5. Only English

B. Topics of Conversation

P: Politics
R: Religion
S: School
M: Medical issues
F: Family issues
C: Childhood or past
D: Dreams and thoughts
O: Other_____ (please explain your answer)

1. Age_____   2. Sex: M   F   3. Place of birth_____ , _____.   4. Age of Arrival to U.S. ___

                                           state   country

5. When you refer to yourself ethnically or culturally, you say that you are_____

6. What year are you in school? _____   7. Are you currently employed? Y   N
                                               (How many hours do you work per week ? _____)

8. What is the highest academic degree you plan to work to achieve in your lifetime? (Circle one choice)
    a. GED   b. High school diploma   c. Vocational school degree d. Junior college degree (2 years)   e. Bachelor's degree (4 years) f. Graduate /Professional degree   g. None of the above

9. After obtaining your highest degree, what do you intend to have as a profession? _____

10. Please answer the following questions about your language skills by circling the appropriate answer.

    a. You first learned to **speak**   Spanish   English Both
    b. You first learned to **read**   Spanish   English Both
    c. You first learned to **write**   Spanish   English Both

    d. You feel that You **speak** Spanish   Excellent   Well   Fair   Poor
    e. You feel that You **understand** Spanish   Excellent   Well   Fair   Poor
    f. You feel that You can **read** Spanish   Excellent   Well   Fair   Poor
    g. You feel that You can **write** Spanish   Excellent   Well   Fair   Poor
    h. You feel that You **speak** English   Excellent   Well   Fair   Poor
    i. You feel that You **understand** English   Excellent   Well   Fair   Poor
    j. You feel that You can **read** English   Excellent   Well   Fair   Poor
    k. You feel that You can **write** English   Excellent   Well   Fair   Poor

11. Please fill in the following chart about your family members with whom you speak frequently. Please mention if they are male or female relatives and use sections A and B from the answer sheet where shown.

to about...	Age (roughly)	Born in (country)	This person speaks...	You speak to this person at home in...	You typically speak this person
			(A)	(A)	(B)
Parents					
Mother	_____	_____	_____	_____	P R S M F C D O__
Father	_____	_____	_____	_____	P R S M F C D O__
Brothers/Sisters					
M F	_____	_____	_____	_____	P R S M F C D O__
M F	_____	_____	_____	_____	P R S M F C D O__
M F	_____	_____	_____	_____	P R S M F C D O__
M F	_____	_____	_____	_____	P R S M F C D O__
M F	_____	_____	_____	_____	P R S M F C D O__
M F	_____	_____	_____	_____	P R S M F C D O__
Cousins					
M F	_____	_____	_____	_____	P R S M F C D O__
M F	_____	_____	_____	_____	P R S M F C D O__
M F	_____	_____	_____	_____	P R S M F C D O__

Aunts/Uncles
  M F   _____ _____ _____   _____   P R S M F C D O__
  M F   _____ _____ _____   _____   P R S M F C D O__
  M F   _____ _____ _____   _____   P R S M F C D O__
Nieces/Nephews
  M F   _____ _____ _____   _____   P R S M F C D O__
  M F   _____ _____ _____   _____   P R S M F C D O__
  M F   _____ _____ _____   _____   P R S M F C D O__
Grandparents
  M F   _____ _____ _____   _____   P R S M F C D O__
  M F   _____ _____ _____   _____   P R S M F C D O__
  M F   _____ _____ _____   _____   P R S M F C D O__
Best Friend
  M F   _____ _____ _____   _____   P R S M F C D O__
  M F   _____ _____ _____   _____   P R S M F C D O__

12. a. Mother's occupation:_____ b. Last grade she completed _____

13. a. Father's occupation:_____ b. Last grade he completed _____

14. How many brothers and sisters do you have that...
      a. ...finished high school and continued studying?   _____
      b. ...finished high school and started working?   _____
      c. ...dropped out of high school and did or is doing the GED? _____
      d. ...dropped out of high school and has not done the GED? _____
      e. ...are older and never went to high school?   _____
      f. ...are now in school?   _____
      g. ...are too young to go to school?   _____

15. Were you ever in a bilingual education program?   Y N
      If yes, what grade levels?_____ Where was/were the school(s)?_____

16. Have you ever taken a class (other than a language class) where the teacher taught
    only in Spanish? Y N
      If yes, what grade levels?_____ Where was/were the school(s)?_____

17. Did you ever repeat a grade? Y N   How many times? _____

18. Please answer the following questions about your **high school experiences** the best that you can.

    a. How would you describe your course work at high school?: (Please check one)
        ____vocational (remedial or basic courses in math/English, home economics, shop, work-
        study)
        ____general (basic courses in math or science, creative writing, etc.)
        ____college preparatory (advanced courses in math, science, rhetoric,literature, history)

    b. What grades do you usually get ? (Circle one choice) A's   A's & B's B's B's & C's C's
                                                             C's & D's D's D's & F's   F's
    c. Do you cut class?   Y N
    d. Have you ever been suspended or put on probation?   Y N
    e. Do you participate in any extracurricular activities offered by your school (sports, clubs)? Y N
    f. Are you popular in school?   Y N
    g. Do you have a positive attitude about yourself? Y   N
    h. Do you feel that you are able to do things as well as most other people?   Y   N
    i. Do you feel that good luck is more important than hard work?   Y   N
    j. Do you feel that others are stopping you from getting ahead?   Y   N

19. How much do your parents...

	Often	Sometimes	Never
a. ...help you with your homework?	___	___	___
b. ...talk about your plans after finishing high school?	___	___	___
c. ...know exactly where you are during non-school hours?	___	___	___

20. How much of your free time do you spend..

	Often	Sometimes	Never
a. studying and doing homework?	___	___	___
b. hanging out with friends?	___	___	___

21. What language do you use most often when you...

	Spanish	English	Both
a. ...watch the news on TV?	___	___	___
b. ...watch other TV programs?	___	___	___
c. ...listen to the radio or music?	___	___	___
d. ...read the newspaper ?	___	___	___
e. ...read magazines?	___	___	___
f. ...read books?	___	___	___

22. What language do you use most often when you...

	Spanish	English	Both
a. ...add up numbers in your head?	___	___	___
b. ...are alone and you're thinking?	___	___	___
c. ...are alone and you're praying?	___	___	___
d. ...are dreaming?	___	___	___

23. What language do you usewhen the person you're speaking to is bilingual...

	Spanish only	Mixed Sp/Eng	English only	Either Sp or Eng
a. ...and you're happy?	___	___	___	___
b. ...and you're mad?	___	___	___	___
c. ...and you're nervous?	___	___	___	___
d. ...and you're sad?	___	___	___	___
e. ...and you're trying to win an argument?	___	___	___	___
f. ...and you're explaining how something mechanical works?	___	___	___	___
g. ...and you're ordering them to do something?	___	___	___	___
h. ...and you talk about home events?	___	___	___	___
i. ...and you gossip about someone?	___	___	___	___
j. ...and you talk about work events?	___	___	___	___
k. ...and you talk about world events?	___	___	___	___

24. The following statements refer to **Spanish**. Please say if you **Agree, Disagree** or are **Undecided**.

a. You prefer to speak Spanish rather than English	**A**	**D**	**U**
b. You feel proud that you speak Spanish	**A**	**D**	**U**
c. You feel lucky that you speak Spanish.	**A**	**D**	**U**
d. It is important to you to be able to speak Spanish .	**A**	**D**	**U**
e. A person can have more job opportunities if they know Spanish .	**A**	**D**	**U**
f. You can communicate with more people by speaking Spanish.	**A**	**D**	**U**
g. Spanish is a useful language to know.	**A**	**D**	**U**
h. Knowing Spanish helps you seem more educated to others.	**A**	**D**	**U**
i. You feel more comfortable around people who speak Spanish.	**A**	**D**	**U**
j. Spanish helps you make friends.	**A**	**D**	**U**
k. Speaking Spanish makes you feel like you belong to a group.	**A**	**D**	**U**
l. Speaking Spanish is an important part of your family life.	**A**	**D**	**U**
m. Speaking Spanish is an important part of your school life.	**A**	**D**	**U**

n.	Speaking Spanish is an important part of your social life.	**A D U**
o.	Bilingual education programs should develop Spanish skills for all students.	**A D U**
p.	Bilingual education programs should develop Spanish skills for Latino students.	**A D U**
q.	Latinos should know Spanish.	**A D U**
r.	Spanish is an essential part of latino culture.	**A D U**
s.	When you have children, you want them to be able to speak Spanish .	**A D U**
t.	Spanish helps our community progress.	**A D U**

25. The following questions refer to **English**. Please mark if you **A**gree, **D**isagree or are **U**ndecided.

a.	You prefer to speak English than Spanish.	**A D U**
b.	You feel proud that you speak English.	**A D U**
c.	You feel lucky that you speak English.	**A D U**
d.	It is important to you to be able to speak English.	**A D U**
e.	A person can have more job opportunities if they know English.	**A D U**
f.	You can communicate with more people by speaking English.	**A D U**
g.	English is a useful language to know.	**A D U**
h.	Knowing English helps you seem more educated to others.	**A D U**
i.	You feel more comfortable around people who speak English.	**A D U**
j.	English helps you make friends.	**A D U**
k.	Speaking English makes you feel like you belong to a group.	**A D U**
l.	Speaking English is an important part of your family life.	**A D U**
m.	Speaking English is an important part of your school life.	**A D U**
n.	Speaking English is an important part of your social life.	**A D U**
o.	Bilingual education programs should develop English skills for Latino students.	**A D U**
p.	Latinos should know English.	**A D U**
q.	English is a threat to latino culture.	**A D U**
r.	English helps our community progress.	**A D U**

26. Please mark which language or languages is/are most appropriate for the following situations.

		Spanish	English	Either
a.	Science	_____	_____	_____
b.	Military commands	_____	_____	_____
c.	Religious rituals	_____	_____	_____
d.	Politics	_____	_____	_____
e.	Novels	_____	_____	_____
f.	Poetry	_____	_____	_____
g.	Folksongs	_____	_____	_____
h.	Bargaining	_____	_____	_____
i.	Joking	_____	_____	_____
j.	Cursing	_____	_____	_____
k.	Speaking to babies	_____	_____	_____
l.	Lying	_____	_____	_____
m.	Persuading	_____	_____	_____

27. For each pair of characteristics, place an X on the line that represents how you feel about the **Spanish** language.

Beautiful	___	___	___	___	___	Ugly
Rich	___	___	___	___	___	Poor
Noisy	___	___	___	___	___	Musical
Precise	___	___	___	___	___	Vague
Illogical	___	___	___	___	___	Logical
Simple	___	___	___	___	___	Sophisticated
Rhythmical	___	___	___	___	___	Irregular
Refined	___	___	___	___	___	Vulgar
Bland	___	___	___	___	___	Colorful
Private	___	___	___	___	___	Public
Superior	___	___	___	___	___	Inferior
Impure	___	___	___	___	___	Pure
Soothing	___	___	___	___	___	Unnerving
Graceful	___	___	___	___	___	Clumsy
Profane	___	___	___	___	___	Sacred

Thank you for your participation

High School Student Questionnaire—Spanish

Instructor _____   No. _____

Urbana, enero de 1995

Estimado/a estudiante:

Como ya le ha mencionado nuestro/a entrevistador/a, estamos haciendo un estudio sobre los jóvenes latinos. Este estudio se está llevando a cabo en el Departamento de Español, Italiano y Portugués de la Universidad de Illinois en Urbana-Champaign. El propósito de nuestro estudio es examinar las características lingüísticas de los jóvenes bilingües de diferentes niveles académicos.

Su participación en este estudio es **VOLUNTARIA** y **ANONIMA**. Si acepta participar, el/la entrevistador/a le ayudará a interpretar las preguntas y le indicará cómo marcar sus respuestas. Usted tiene la libertad de no responder a aquellas preguntas que le parezcan ofensivas. La entrevista toma menos de 45 minutos para completar.

Le agradecemos por su interés en nuestro estudio.

Hoja de Respuestas

A. Idioma que se usa:

1. Solamente español
2. Mayormente español, pero mezclado con inglés
3. A veces solamente español, a veces solamente inglés
4. Mayormente inglés, pero mezclado con español
5. Solamente inglés

B. Temas de Conversación

P: la Política
R: la Religión
S: la eScuela
M: Asuntos Médicos
F: Asuntos Familiares
C: Cuando era niño/a o el pasado
D: Deseos y pensamientos
O: Otro_____ (favor de clarificar su respuesta)

1. Edad____ 2. Sexo: M F 3. Lugar de nacimiento_____ , _____ 4. Edad de llegada a USA___

estado   país

5. Cuando Ud. se refiere a sí mismo de manera étnica o cultural, Ud. dice que es _____

6. ¿En qué grado está? _____   7. ¿Tiene trabajo ahora? Sí   No

¿Cuántas horas trabaja a la semana? _____

8. ¿Cuál es el título académico más avanzado que Ud. espera conseguir? (Circule una opción)
   a. GED   b. diploma de la secundaria   c. diploma vocacional
   d. diploma de un colegio comunitario (2 años)   e. diploma universitario (4 años)
   f. maestría, doctorado   g. ninguno

9. Al conseguir su título más avanzado, ¿qué ocupación desea desempeñar? _____

10. Favor de contestar las preguntas a continuación. Haga un círculo a la respuesta más apropiada.

a. Ud. aprendió primero a **hablar** en	Español	Inglés	Ambos
b. Ud. aprendió primero a **leer** en	Español	Inglés	Ambos
c. Ud. aprendió primero a **escribir** en	Español	Inglés	Ambos
d. Ud. considera que **habla** español	Excelente	Bien	Regular	Mal
e. Ud. considera que **entiende** español	Excelente	Bien	Regular	Mal
f. Ud. considera que puede **leer** español	Excelente	Bien	Regular	Mal
g. Ud. considera que puede **escribir** español	Excelente	Bien	Regular	Mal
h. Ud. considera que **habla** inglés	Excelente	Bien	Regular	Mal
i. Ud. considera que **entiende** inglés	Excelente	Bien	Regular	Mal
j. Ud. considera que puede **leer** Inglés	Excelente	Bien	Regular	Mal
k. Ud. considera que puede **escribir** Inglés	Excelente	Bien	Regular	Mal

11. Favor de llenar la tabla abajo sobre los miembros de su familia y amigos con quienes habla con frecuencia. Mencione si la persona es masculina o femenina y utilice las secciones A y B de la hoja de respuestas según se indique.

habla con	Edad	Nació en	Esta persona	En casa Ud. le	Tipicamente, Ud.
sobre... (B)	(aproximada) (país)		habla... (A)	habla en...(A)	esta persona
Padres					
Madre	_____	_____	_____	_____	P R S M F C D O_
Padre	_____	_____	_____	_____	P R S M F C D O_
Hermanos					
M F	_____	_____	_____	_____	P R S M F C D O_
M F	_____	_____	_____	_____	P R S M F C D O_
M F	_____	_____	_____	_____	P R S M F C D O_
M F	_____	_____	_____	_____	P R S M F C D O_
M F	_____	_____	_____	_____	P R S M F C D O_
M F	_____	_____	_____	_____	P R S M F C D O_
Primos					
M F	_____	_____	_____	_____	P R S M F C D O_
M F	_____	_____	_____	_____	P R S M F C D O_
M F	_____	_____	_____	_____	P R S M F C D O_
Tíos					
M F	_____	_____	_____	_____	P R S M F C D O_
M F	_____	_____	_____	_____	P R S M F C D O_
M F	_____	_____	_____	_____	P R S M F C D O_

Sobrinos
M F _____ _____ ____ ____ P R S M F C D O_
M F _____ _____ ____ ____ P R S M F C D O_
M F _____ _____ ____ ____ P R S M F C D O_
Abuelos
M F _____ _____ ____ ____ P R S M F C D O_
M F _____ _____ ____ ____ P R S M F C D O_
M F _____ _____ ____ ____ P R S M F C D O_
Mejores Amigos
M F _____ _____ ____ ____ P R S M F C D O_
M F _____ _____ ____ ____ P R S M F C D O_

12. a. Ocupación de su madre:_____ b. Ultimo grado que ella terminó _____

13. a. Ocupación de su padre:_____ b. Ultimo grado que él terminó _____

14. ¿Cuántos hermanos/as tiene Ud. que...
    a. ...terminaron la secundaria y siguieron estudiando? _____
    b. ...terminaron la secundaria y empezaron a trabajar? _____
    c. ...dejaron la secundaria y sacaron o están sacando el GED? _____
    d. ...dejaron la secundaria y no sacaron o ni están sacando el GED? _____
    e. ...son adultos y nunca fueron a la secundaria? _____
    f. ...asisten todavía a escuelas primarias o secundarias _____
    g. ...son todavía demasiado pequeños para asistir a la escuela? _____

15. ¿Participó Ud. alguna vez en un programa bilingüe? Sí No
    Si responde que sí, ¿en qué grado(s)?_____ ¿Dónde fue(ron) la(s) escuela(s)?_____

16. ¿Ha tomado alguna vez un curso (que no sea de idiomas) donde el maestro enseñaba en español?
    Sí No
    Si responde que sí, ¿en qué grado(s)?_____ ¿Dónde fue(ron) la(s) escuela(s)?_____

17. ¿Repitió alguna vez algún grado? Sí No ¿Cuántas veces ha repetido grado(s)? _____

18. Conteste las siguientes preguntas sobre sus **experiencias en la secundaria** lo mejor que pueda.

    a. Como describiría sus cursos en la secundaria: (Marcar uno)
       ____vocacionales (cursos básicos/remediales de matemáticas, inglés, estudios domésticos,
       talleres)
       ____generales (cursos básicos de matemáticas, ciencias; composición básica)
       ____preparatorios para la universidad (cursos avanzados de matemáticas, ciencias;
       retórica, literatura)

    b. ¿Qué calificaciones saca Ud.? (Circule una respuesta) A's A's y B's B's B's y C's C's
       C's y D's D's D's y F's F's
    c. ¿Se va Ud. de pinta (falta a clases voluntariamente)? Sí No
    d. ¿Alguna vez fue suspendido o puesto bajo probación? Sí No
    e. ¿Participa en actividades extracurriculares ofrecidas por la escuela (deportes/ clubs)? Sí No
    f. ¿Es Ud. popular en la escuela? Sí No
    g. ¿Tiene Ud. una actitud positiva hacia sí mismo? Sí No
    h. ¿Siente Ud. que tiene igual capacidad que cualquier otra persona para hacer
       cualquier cosa? Sí No
    i. ¿Siente Ud. que la buena suerte es más importante que el trabajo duro? Sí No
    j. ¿Siente Ud. que hay personas que le impiden progresar? Sí No

19. Sus padres,...   A menudo   A veces   Nunca
    a. ¿cuánto le ayudan a Ud. con la tarea?
    b. ¿cuánto le hablan de sus planes de cuando termine la secundaria?   _____   _____   _____
    c. ¿saben exactamente donde encontrarlo/la después de clases?   _____   _____   _____

20. ¿Cómo pasa su tiempo libre?   A menudo   A veces   Nunca
    a. ¿estudiando y haciendo la tarea?
    b. ¿con sus amigos?   _____   _____   _____

21. ¿Qué lengua usa más frecuentemente cuando...

	Español	Inglés	Ambos
a. ...mira las noticias?			
b. ...mira otros programas de televisión?	_____	_____	_____
c. ...escucha la radio o música ?			
d. ...lee el periódico ?	_____	_____	_____
e. ...lee revistas ?			
f. ...lee libros?	_____	_____	_____

22. ¿Qué lengua usa más frecuentemente cuando...

	Español	Inglés	Ambos
a. ...suma números mentalmente?	_____	_____	_____
b. ...está solo y piensa?			
c. ...está solo y reza?	_____	_____	_____
d. ...sueña ?			

23. ¿Qué lengua usa cuando la persona con quien está hablando es bilingüe y..

	Sólo Español	Es/Ing Mezclado	Sólo Inglés	O Esp o Ing.
a. ...Ud. está contento?				
b. ...Ud. está enojado?	_____	_____	_____	_____
c. ...Ud. está nervioso?				
d. ...Ud. está triste?	_____	_____	_____	_____
e. ...Ud. está tratando de ganarle una discusión?				
f. ...Ud. está explicándole cómo funciona algo mecánico?	_____	_____	_____	_____
g. ...Ud. le está ordenando hacer algo?				
h. ...Ud. le habla de temas familiares?	_____	_____	_____	_____
i. ...Ud. le chismea de alguien?				
j. ...Ud. le habla de cosas del trabajo?	_____	_____	_____	_____
k. ...Ud. le habla de eventos mundiales?	_____	_____	_____	_____

24. Las siguientes oraciones se refieren al **español**. Responda o de Acuerdo, en Desacuerdo, o Indeciso.

	A	D	I
a. Ud. prefiere hablar español más que inglés.	A	D	I
b. Ud. se siente orgulloso de hablar español	A	D	I
c. Ud. se siente afortunado de hablar español.	A	D	I
d. Es importante para Ud. poder hablar español .	A	D	I
e. Uno tiene más oportunidades de empleo si sabe español.	A	D	I
f. Uno puede comunicarse con más gente si sabe español.	A	D	I
g. El español es un idioma útil.	A	D	I
h. El saber español hace que otros lo vean como más culto (educado).	A	D	I
i. Se siente más cómodo con gente que habla español.	A	D	I
j. El español le ayuda a hacer amigos.	A	D	I
k. El hablar español hace sentirse que forma parte de un grupo.	A	D	I
l. El hablar español es importante para su vida familiar.	A	D	I

m. El hablar español es importante para su vida escolar	A	D	I
n. El hablar español es importante para su vida social	A	D	I
o. La educación bilingüe debe ayudar a todos a desarrollar sus habilidades en español.	A	D	I
p. La educación bilingüe debe ayudar a los latinos a desarrollar sus habilidades en español	A	D	I
q. Los latinos deben saber español.	A	D	I
r. El español es una parte importante de la cultura latina.	A	D	I
s. Cuando tenga hijos, Ud. quiere que aprendan español .	A	D	I
t. El español ayuda a nuestra comunidad a progresar.	A	D	I

25. Las siguientes oraciones se refieren al **inglés**, responda o de Acuerdo, en Desacuerdo, o Indeciso.

a. Ud. prefiere hablar inglés más que español.	A	D	I
b. Ud. se siente orgulloso de hablar inglés	A	D	I
c. Ud. se siente afortunado de hablar inglés.	A	D	I
d. Es importante para Ud. poder hablar inglés .	A	D	I
e. Uno tiene más oportunidades de empleo si sabe inglés.	A	D	I
f. Uno puede comunicarse con más gente si sabe inglés.	A	D	I
g. El inglés es un idioma útil.	A	D	I
h. El saber inglés hace que otros lo vean como más culto (educado).	A	D	I
i. Se siente más cómodo con gente que habla inglés.	A	D	I
j. El inglés le ayuda a hacer amigos.	A	D	I
k. El hablar inglés le hace sentir seque forma parte de un grupo.	A	D	I
l. El hablar inglés es importante para su vida familiar.	A	D	I
m. El hablar inglés es importante para su vida escolar.	A	D	I
n. El hablar inglés es importante para su vida social.	A	D	I
o. La educación bilingüe debe ayudar a los latinos a desarrollar sus habilidades en inglés.	A	D	I
p. Los latinos deben saber inglés.	A	D	I
q. El inglés es una amenaza a la cultura latina.	A	D	I
r. El inglés ayuda a nuestra comunidad a progresar.	A	D	I

26. Favor de mencionar qué idioma(s) cree Ud. que es (son) más apropiado(s) para las siguientes situaciones.

	Español	Inglés	Cualquiera de los dos
a. la ciencia	____	____	____
b. las órdenes militares	____	____	____
c. los ritos religiosos	____	____	____
d. la política	____	____	____
e. las novelas	____	____	____
f. la poesía	____	____	____
g. la música folklórica	____	____	____
h. el regateo	____	____	____
i. las bromas	____	____	____
j. las maldiciones	____	____	____
k. el hablar con niños	____	____	____
l. el mentir	____	____	____
m. el persuadir	____	____	____

27. Para cada par de características, marque con una X en la escala cómo se siente Ud. hacia el **español**.

Bonito	____	____	____	____	____	Feo
Rico	____	____	____	____	____	Pobre
Ruidoso	____	____	____	____	____	Musical
Preciso	____	____	____	____	____	Vago
Ilógico	____	____	____	____	____	Lógico
Sencillo	____	____	____	____	____	Sofisticado
Rítmico	____	____	____	____	____	Irregular
Refinado	____	____	____	____	____	Vulgar
Sin color	____	____	____	____	____	Colorido
Privado	____	____	____	____	____	Público
Superior	____	____	____	____	____	Inferior
No puro	____	____	____	____	____	Puro
Tranquilo	____	____	____	____	____	Nervioso
Agil	____	____	____	____	____	Torpe
Común	____	____	____	____	____	Sagrado

Gracias por su participación

College Student Questionnaire—
English

Urbana, April 1995

Dear Student:

As has been mentioned to you by the researcher, we are conducting a study on Latino/a students. This study is being conducted at the Department of Spanish, Italian and Portugu at the University of Illinois at Urbana-Champaign. The purpose of our study is to explore th language characteristics of bilingual youths at different academic levels.

Your participation is **VOLUNTARY** and strictly **ANONYMOUS**. If you agree to participate, t researcher will guide you through the survey and instruct you on how to mark your answers You are free not to answer questions you might feel offend you. The interview will take no than 45 minutes to complete.

Thank you for your interest in our study.

Answer Guide

A. Language used:

1. Spanish only
2. Mostly Spanish, but mixed with some English
3. Sometimes only Spanish, sometimes only English
4. Mostly English, but mixed with some Spanish
5. Only English

B. Topics of Conversation

P: Politics
R: Religion
S: School
M: Medical issues
F: Family issues
C: Childhood or past
D: Dreams and thoughts
O: Other_____ (please explain your answer)

1. Age_____   2. Sex: M   F   3. Place of birth_____ , _____.   4. Age of Arrival to U.S. ___
                                                      state   country
5. When you refer to yourself ethnically or culturally, you say that you are_____

6a. What year are you in college? _____   b. Current major _____   Current GPA_____/5.0

7. Are you currently employed? Y   N   (How many hours do you work per week ? _____)

8. What is the highest academic degree you plan to work to achieve in your lifetime? (Circle one choice)
   a. GED   b. High school diploma   c. Vocational school degree
   d. Junior college degree (2 years)   e. Bachelor's degree (4 years)
   f. Graduate /Professional degree   g. None of the above

9. After obtaining your highest degree, what do you intend to have as a profession? _____

10. Please answer the following questions about your language skills by circling the appropriate answer.

   a. You first learned to **speak**   Spanish   English Both
   b. You first learned to **read**   Spanish   English Both
   c. You first learned to **write**   Spanish   English Both

   d. You feel that You **speak** Spanish   Excellent   Well   Fair   Poor
   e. You feel that You **understand** Spanish   Excellent   Well   Fair   Poor
   f. You feel that You can **read** Spanish   Excellent   Well   Fair   Poor
   g. You feel that You can **write** Spanish   Excellent   Well   Fair   Poor
   h. You feel that You **speak** English   Excellent   Well   Fair   Poor
   i. You feel that You **understand** English   Excellent   Well   Fair   Poor
   j. You feel that You can **read** English   Excellent   Well   Fair   Poor
   k. You feel that You can **write** English   Excellent   Well   Fair   Poor

11.   Please fill in the following chart about your family members with whom you speak frequently.
Please mention
    if they are male or female relatives and use sections A and B from the answer sheet where shown.

	Age	Born in	This person	You speak to this	You typically speak
to this					
	(roughly)	(country)	speaks... (A)	person at home in... (A)	person about... (B)
Parents					
Mother	_____	_____	_____	_____	P R S M F C D O_
Father	_____	_____	_____	_____	P R S M F C D O_
Brothers/Sisters					
M F	_____	_____	_____	_____	P R S M F C D O_
M F	_____	_____	_____	_____	P R S M F C D O_
M F	_____	_____	_____	_____	P R S M F C D O_
M F	_____	_____	_____	_____	P R S M F C D O_
M F	_____	_____	_____	_____	P R S M F C D O_
Cousins					
M F	_____	_____	_____	_____	P R S M F C D O_
M F	_____	_____	_____	_____	P R S M F C D O_
M F	_____	_____	_____	_____	P R S M F C D O_
Aunts/Uncles					
M F	_____	_____	_____	_____	P R S M F C D O_
M F	_____	_____	_____	_____	P R S M F C D O_
M F	_____	_____	_____	_____	P R S M F C D O_

Nieces/Nephews

M F	_____	_____	_____	_____	P R S M F C D O_
M F	_____	_____	_____	_____	P R S M F C D O_
M F	_____	_____	_____	_____	P R S M F C D O_

Grandparents

M F	_____	_____	_____	_____	P R S M F C D O_
M F	_____	_____	_____	_____	P R S M F C D O_
M F	_____	_____	_____	_____	P R S M F C D O_

Best Friend

| M F | _____ | _____ | _____ | _____ | P R S M F C D O_ |
| M F | _____ | _____ | _____ | _____ | P R S M F C D O_ |

12 a Mother's occupation: _____   b Last grade she completed _____

13 a Father's occupation: _____   b Last grade he completed _____

14 How many brothers and sisters do you have that
- a ...finished high school and continued studying? _____
- b ...finished high school and started working? _____
- c ...dropped out of high school and did or is doing the GED? _____
- d ...dropped out of high school and has not done the GED? _____
- e ...are older and never went to high school? _____
- f ...are now in school? _____
- g ...are too young to go to school? _____

15. Were you ever in a bilingual education program?   Y N
      If yes, what grade levels?_____ Where was/were the school(s)?_____

16. Have you ever taken a class (other than a language class) where the teacher taught only in Spanish?
      Y N
      If yes, what grade levels?_____ Where was/were the school(s)?_____

17. Did you ever repeat a grade?   Y N   How many times? _____

Please answer questions 18-20 about your **high school experiences** the best that you can.

18. What high school(s) did you attend and where? _____   _____
                                                                    school(s)   city

a. How would you describe your course work at high school?: (Please check one)
         ____vocational (remedial or basic courses in math/English, home economics, shop, work-
               study)
         ____general (basic courses in math or science, creative writing, etc.)
         ____college preparatory (advanced courses in math, science, rhetoric,literature, history)

b. What grades did you usually get ? (Circle one choice) A's   A's & B's B's   B's & C's C's
                                                                    C's & D's D's   D's & F's F's

c. Did you cut class?   Y N
d. Were you ever suspended or put on probation? Y N
e. Did you participate in any extracurricular activities offered by your school (sports, clubs)? Y N
f. Were you popular in school?   Y N
g. Did you have a positive attitude about yourself? Y N
h. Did you feel that you were able to do things as well as most other people?   Y N
i. Did you feel that good luck was more important than hard work? Y N
j. Did you feel that others were stopping you from getting ahead? Y N

19. How much did your parents...

	Often	Sometimes	Never
a. ...help you with your homework?	___	___	___
b. ...talk about your plans after finishing high school?	___	___	___
c. ...know exactly where you were during non-school hours?	___	___	___

20. How much of your free time did you spend..

	Often	Sometimes	Never
a. studying and doing homework?	___	___	___
b. hanging out with friends?	___	___	___

21. When you have access to media in both Spanish and English, what language do you use most often when you...

	Spanish	English	Both
a. ...watch the news on TV?	___	___	___
b. ...watch other TV programs?	___	___	___
c. ...listen to the radio or music?	___	___	___
d. ...read the newspaper ?	___	___	___
e. ...read magazines?	___	___	___
f. ...read books?	___	___	___

22. What language do you use most often when you...

	Spanish	English	Both
a. ...add up numbers in your head?	___	___	___
b. ...are alone and you're thinking?	___	___	___
c. ...are alone and you're praying?	___	___	___
d. ...are dreaming?	___	___	___

23. What language do you use when the person you're speaking to is bilingual...

	Spanish only	Mixed Sp/Eng	English only	Either Sp or Eng
a. ...and you're happy?	___	___	___	___
b. ...and you're mad?	___	___	___	___
c. ...and you're nervous?	___	___	___	___
d. ...and you're sad?	___	___	___	___
e. ...and you're trying to win an argument?	___	___	___	___
f. ...and you're explaining how something mechanical works?	___	___	___	___
g. ...and you're ordering them to do something?	___	___	___	___
h. ...and you talk about home events?	___	___	___	___
i. ...and you gossip about someone?	___	___	___	___
j. ...and you talk about work events?	___	___	___	___
k. ...and you talk about world events?	___	___	___	___

24. The following statements refer to **Spanish**. Please say if you **A**gree, **D**isagree or are **U**ndecided.

a. You prefer to speak Spanish rather than English	A	D	U
b. You feel proud that you speak Spanish	A	D	U
c. You feel lucky that you speak Spanish.	A	D	U
d. It is important to you to be able to speak Spanish .	A	D	U
e. A person can have more job opportunities if they know Spanish .	A	D	U
f. You can communicate with more people by speaking Spanish.	A	D	U
g. Spanish is a useful language to know.	A	D	U
h. Knowing Spanish helps you seem more educated to others.	A	D	U
i. You feel more comfortable around people who speak Spanish.	A	D	U
j. Spanish helps you make friends.	A	D	U
k. Speaking Spanish makes you feel like you belong to a group.	A	D	U
l. Speaking Spanish is an important part of your family life.	A	D	U
m. Speaking Spanish is an important part of your school life.	A	D	U

n. Speaking Spanish is an important part of your social life.   **A   D   U**

o. Bilingual education programs should develop
Spanish skills for all students.   **A   D   U**

p. Bilingual education programs should develop
Spanish skills for Latino students.   **A   D   U**

q. Latinos should know Spanish.   **A   D   U**

r. Spanish is an essential part of Latino culture.   **A   D   U**

s. When you have children, you want them to be able to speak Spanish .   **A   D   U**

t. Spanish helps our community progress.   **A   D   U**

25. The following questions refer to **English**. Please mark if you **A**gree, **D**isagree or are **U**ndecided.

a. You prefer to speak English than Spanish.   **A   D   U**

b. You feel proud that you speak English.   **A   D   U**

c. You feel lucky that you speak English.   **A   D   U**

d. It is important to you to be able to speak English.   **A   D   U**

e. A person can have more job opportunities if they know English.   **A   D   U**

f. You can communicate with more people by speaking English.   **A   D   U**

g. English is a useful language to know.   **A   D   U**

h. Knowing English helps you seem more educated to others.   **A   D   U**

i. You feel more comfortable around people who speak English.   **A   D   U**

j. English helps you make friends.   **A   D   U**

k. Speaking English makes you feel like you belong to a group.   **A   D   U**

l. Speaking English is an important part of your family life.   **A   D   U**

m. Speaking English is an important part of your school life.   **A   D   U**

n. Speaking English is an important part of your social life.   **A   D   U**

o. Bilingual education programs should develop
English skills for Latino students.   **A   D   U**

p. Latinos should know English.   **A   D   U**

q. English is a threat to Latino culture.   **A   D   U**

r. English helps our community progress.   **A   D   U**

26. Please mark which language or languages is/are most appropriate for the following situations.

	Spanish	English	Either
a. Science	_____	_____	_____
b. Military commands	_____	_____	_____
c. Religious rituals	_____	_____	_____
d. Politics	_____	_____	_____
e. Novels	_____	_____	_____
f. Poetry	_____	_____	_____
g. Folksongs	_____	_____	_____
h. Bargaining	_____	_____	_____
i. Joking	_____	_____	_____
j. Cursing	_____	_____	_____
k. Speaking to babies	_____	_____	_____
l. Lying	_____	_____	_____
m. Persuading	_____	_____	_____

27. For each pair of characteristics, place an X on the line that represents how you feel about the **Spanish** language.

Beautiful	___	___	___	___	___	Ugly
Rich	___	___	___	___	___	Poor
Noisy	___	___	___	___	___	Musical
Precise	___	___	___	___	___	Vague
Illogical	___	___	___	___	___	Logical
Simple	___	___	___	___	___	Sophisticated
Rhythmical	___	___	___	___	___	Irregular
Refined	___	___	___	___	___	Vulgar
Bland	___	___	___	___	___	Colorful
Private	___	___	___	___	___	Public
Superior	___	___	___	___	___	Inferior
Impure	___	___	___	___	___	Pure
Soothing	___	___	___	___	___	Unnerving
Graceful	___	___	___	___	___	Clumsy
Profane	___	___	___	___	___	Sacred

Thank you for your participation

College Student Questionnaire—
Spanish

Urbana, abril de 1995

Estimado/a estudiante:

Como ya le ha mencionado nuestro/a entrevistador/a, estamos haciendo un estudio sobre los jóvenes latinos. Este estudio se está llevando a cabo en el Departamento de Español, Italiano y Portugués de la Universidad de Illinois en Urbana-Champaign. El propósito de nuestro estudio es examinar las características lingüísticas de los jóvenes bilingües de diferentes niveles académicos.

Su participación en este estudio es **VOLUNTARIA** y **ANONIMA**. Si acepta participar, el/la entrevistador/a le ayudará a interpretar las preguntas y le indicará cómo marcar sus respuestas. Usted tiene la libertad de no responder a aquellas preguntas que le parezcan ofensivas. La entrevista toma menos de 45 minutos para completar.

Le agradecemos por su interés en nuestro estudio.

Hoja de Respuestas

A. Idioma que se usa:

1. Solamente español
2. Mayormente español, pero mezclado con inglés
3. A veces solamente español, a veces solamente inglés
4. Mayormente inglés, pero mezclado con español
5. Solamente inglés

B. Temas de Conversación

P: la **P**olítica
R: la **R**eligión
S: la e**S**cuela
M: Asuntos **M**édicos
F: Asuntos **F**amiliares
C: **C**uando era niño/a o el pasado
D: **D**eseos y pensamientos
O: **O**tro_____ (favor de clarificar su respuesta)

1. Edad_____ 2. Sexo: M   F 3. Lugar de nacimiento___ , _____ 4. Edad de llegada a USA____
                                            estado   país

5. Cuando Ud. se refiere a sí mismo de manera étnica o cultural, Ud. dice que es _____

6. a. ¿En qué año está? _____ b. ¿Cuál es su concentración _____?   c. ¿Y su GPA? ___/5.0

7. ¿Tiene trabajo ahora? Sí   No   ¿Cuántas horas trabaja a la semana? _____

8. ¿Cuál es el <u>título académico</u> más avanzado que Ud. espera conseguir? (Circule una opción)
      a. GED   b. diploma de la secundaria   c. diploma vocacional
      d. diploma de un colegio comunitario (2 años)   e. diploma universitario (4 años)
      f. maestría, doctorado   g. ninguno

9. Al conseguir su título más avanzado, ¿qué ocupación desea desempeñar? _____

10. Favor de contestar las preguntas a continuación. Haga un círculo a la respuesta más apropiada.
      a. Ud. aprendió primero a **hablar** en   Español   Inglés   Ambos
      b. Ud. aprendió primero a **leer** en   Español   Inglés   Ambos
      c. Ud. aprendió primero a **escribir** en   Español   Inglés   Ambos

      d. Ud. considera que **habla** español   Excelente   Bien   Regular   Mal
      e. Ud. considera que **entiende** español   Excelente   Bien   Regular   Mal
      f. Ud. considera que puede **leer** español   Excelente   Bien   Regular   Mal
      g. Ud. considera que puede **escribir** español   Excelente   Bien   Regular   Mal
      h. Ud. considera que **habla** inglés   Excelente   Bien   Regular   Mal
      i. Ud. considera que **entiende** inglés   Excelente   Bien   Regular   Mal
      j. Ud. considera que puede **leer** Inglés   Excelente   Bien   Regular   Mal
      k. Ud. considera que puede **escribir** Inglés   Excelente   Bien   Regular   Mal

11. Favor de llenar la tabla abajo sobre los miembros de su familia y amigos <u>con quienes habla con frecuencia</u>. Mencione si la persona es masculina o femenina y utilice las secciones A y B de la hoja de respuestas según se indique.

	Edad (aproximada)	Nació en (país)	Esta persona habla... (A)	En casa Ud. le habla en...(A)	Típicamente, Ud. habla con esta persona sobre. (B)
Padres					
Madre	_____	_____	_____	_____	P R S M F C D O_
Padre	_____	_____	_____	_____	P R S M F C D O_
Hermanos					
M F	_____	_____	_____	_____	P R S M F C D O_
M F	_____	_____	_____	_____	P R S M F C D O_
M F	_____	_____	_____	_____	P R S M F C D O_
M F	_____	_____	_____	_____	P R S M F C D O_
M F	_____	_____	_____	_____	P R S M F C D O_
M F	_____	_____	_____	_____	P R S M F C D O_
Primos					
M F	_____	_____	_____	_____	P R S M F C D O_
M F	_____	_____	_____	_____	P R S M F C D O_
M F	_____	_____	_____	_____	P R S M F C D O_
Tíos					
M F	_____	_____	_____	_____	P R S M F C D O_
M F	_____	_____	_____	_____	P R S M F C D O_
M F	_____	_____	_____	_____	P R S M F C D O_

Sobrinos
M F	____	____	____	____	P R S M F C D O_
M F	____	____	____	____	P R S M F C D O_
M F	____	____	____	____	P R S M F C D O_

Abuelos
M F	____	____	____	____	P R S M F C D O_
M F	____	____	____	____	P R S M F C D O_
M F	____	____	____	____	P R S M F C D O_

Mejores Amigos
M F	____	____	____	____	P R S M F C D O_
M F	____	____	____	____	P R S M F C D O_
M F	____	____	____	____	P R S M F C D O_

12. a. Ocupación de su madre:_____   b. Ultimo grado que ella terminó _____

13. a. Ocupación de su padre:_____   b. Ultimo grado que él terminó _____

14. ¿Cuántos hermanos/as tiene Ud. que...
    a. ...terminaron la secundaria y siguieron estudiando?   _____
    b. ...terminaron la secundaria y empezaron a trabajar?   _____
    c. ...dejaron la secundaria y sacaron o están sacando el GED?   _____
    d. ...dejaron la secundaria y no sacaron o ni están sacando el GED?   _____
    e. ...son adultos y nunca fueron a la secundaria?   _____
    f. ...asisten todavía a escuelas primarias o secundarias   _____
    g. ...son todavía demasiado pequeños para asistir a la escuela?   _____

15. ¿Participó Ud. alguna vez en un programa bilingüe?   Sí No
    Si responde que sí, ¿en qué grado(s)?_____ ¿Dónde fue(ron) la(s) escuela(s)?_____

16. ¿Ha tomado alguna vez un curso (que no sea de idiomas) donde el maestro enseñaba en español?
Sí No
    Si responde que sí, ¿en qué grado(s)?_____ ¿Dónde fue(ron) la(s) escuela(s)?_____

17. ¿Repitió alguna vez algún grado?   Sí No   ¿Cuántas veces ha repetido grado(s)? _____

Conteste las preguntas 18-20 sobre sus **experiencias en la secundaria** lo mejor que pueda.
18. ¿A qué escuela(s) asistió y en qué ciudad se encontraba(n)? _____   _____
                                    escuela(s)   ciudad
    a. Como describiría sus cursos en la secundaria: (Marcar uno)
          ____vocacionales (cursos básicos/remediales de matemáticas, inglés, estudios domésticos, talleres)
          ____generales (cursos básicos de matemáticas, ciencias; composición básica)
          ____preparatorios para la universidad (cursos avanzados de matemáticas, ciencias; retórica, literatura)

    b. ¿Qué calificaciones sacaba Ud.? (Circule una respuesta)   A's   A's y B's   B's   B's y C's   C's
                                                  C's y D's   D's   D's y F's   F's

    c. ¿Alguna vez se fue Ud. de pinta (faltó a clases voluntariamente)?   Sí No
    d. ¿Alguna vez fue suspendido o puesto bajo probación?   Sí No
    e. ¿Alguna vez participó en actividades extracurriculares ofrecidas por la escuela
        (deportes/ clubs)? Sí No
    f. ¿Era Ud. popular en la escuela?   Sí No
    g. ¿Tenía Ud. una actitud positiva hacia sí mismo? Sí No
    h. ¿Se sentía con igual capacidad que cualquier otra persona?   Sí No

   i. ¿Sentía Ud. que la buena suerte era más importante que el trabajo?   Sí   No
   j. ¿Sentía Ud. que otros le impedían progresar?   Sí   No

19. Sus padres,...   A menudo A veces   Nunca
     a. ¿cuánto le ayudaban a Ud. con la tarea?
     b. ¿cuánto le hablaban de sus planes de cuando terminara la secundaria?
     c. ¿sabían exactamente donde encontrarlo/la después de clases?

20. ¿Cómo pasaba su tiempo libre?   A menudo A veces   Nunca
     a. ¿estudiando y haciendo la tarea?
     b. ¿con sus amigos?

21. Cuando tiene acceso a medios de comunicación en ambos idiomas, ¿qué lengua usa más frecuentemente cuando...

	Español	Inglés	Ambos
a. ...mira las noticias?			
b. ...mira otros programas de televisión?			
c. ...escucha la radio o música ?			
d. ...lee el periódico ?			
e. ...lee revistas ?			
f. ...lee libros?			

22. ¿Qué lengua usa más frecuentemente cuando...

	Español	Inglés	Ambos
a. ...suma números mentalmente?			
b. ...está solo y piensa?			
c. ...está solo y reza?			
d. ...sueña ?			

23. ¿Qué lengua usa cuando la persona con quien está hablando es bilingüe y..

	Sólo Español	Es/Ing Mezclado	Sólo Inglés	O Esp o Ing.
a. ...Ud. está contento?				
b. ...Ud. está enojado?				
c. ...Ud. está nervioso?				
d. ...Ud. está triste?				
e. ...Ud. está tratando de ganarle una discusión?				
f. ...Ud. está explicándole cómo funciona algo mecánico?				
g. ...Ud. le está ordenando hacer algo?				
h. ...Ud. le habla de temas familiares?				
i. ...Ud. le chismea de alguien?				
j. ...Ud. le habla de cosas del trabajo?				
k. ...Ud. le habla de eventos mundiales?				

24. Las siguientes oraciones se refieren al **español**. Responda o de Acuerdo, en Desacuerdo, o Indeciso.

a. Ud. prefiere hablar español más que inglés.	A	D	I
b. Ud. se siente orgulloso de hablar español.	A	D	I
c. Ud. se siente afortunado de hablar español.	A	D	I
d. Es importante para Ud. poder hablar español .	A	D	I
e. Uno tiene más oportunidades de empleo si sabe español.	A	D	I
f. Uno puede comunicarse con más gente si sabe español.	A	D	I
g. El español es un idioma útil.	A	D	I

h. El saber español hace que otros lo vean como más culto (educado).   A   D   I
i. Se siente más cómodo con gente que habla español.   A   D   I
j. El español le ayuda a hacer amigos.   A   D   I
k. El hablar español hace sentirse que forma parte de un grupo.   A   D   I
l. El hablar español es importante para su vida familiar.   A   D   I
m. El hablar español es importante para su vida escolar.   A   D   I
n. El hablar español es importante para su vida social.   A   D   I
o. La educación bilingüe debe ayudar a todos a desarrollar sus
habilidades en español.   A   D   I
p. La educación bilingüe debe ayudar a los latinos a desarrollar sus
habilidades en español   A   D   I
q. Los latinos deben saber español.   A   D   I
r. El español es una parte importante de la cultura latina.   A   D   I
s. Cuando tenga hijos, Ud. quiere que aprendan español .   A   D   I
t. El español ayuda a nuestra comunidad a progresar.   A   D   I

25. Las siguientes oraciones se refieren al **inglés**, responda o de Acuerdo, en Desacuerdo, o Indeciso.

a. Ud. prefiere hablar inglés más que español.   A   D   I
b. Ud. se siente orgulloso de hablar inglés   A   D   I
c. Ud. se siente afortunado de hablar inglés.   A   D   I
d. Es importante para Ud. poder hablar inglés .   A   D   I
e. Uno tiene más oportunidades de empleo si sabe inglés.   A   D   I
f. Uno puede comunicarse con más gente si sabe inglés.   A   D   I
g. El inglés es un idioma útil.   A   D   I
h. El saber inglés hace que otros lo vean como más culto (educado).   A   D   I
i. Se siente más cómodo con gente que habla inglés.   A   D   I
j. El inglés le ayuda a hacer amigos.   A   D   I
k. El hablar inglés le hace sentir seque forma parte de un grupo.   A   D   I
l. El hablar inglés es importante para su vida familiar.   A   D   I
m. El hablar inglés es importante para su vida escolar.   A   D   I
n. El hablar inglés es importante para su vida social.   A   D   I
o. La educación bilingüe debe ayudar a los latinos a desarrollar sus
habilidades en inglés.   A   D   I
p. Los latinos deben saber inglés.   A   D   I
q. El inglés es una amenaza a la cultura latina.   A   D   I
r. El inglés ayuda a nuestra comunidad a progresar.   A   D   I

26. Favor de mencionar qué idioma(s) cree Ud. que es (son) más apropiado(s) para las siguientes situaciones.

	Español	Inglés	Cualquiera de los dos
a. la ciencia	_____	_____	_____
b. las órdenes militares	_____	_____	_____
c. los ritos religiosos	_____	_____	_____
d. la política	_____	_____	_____
e. las novelas	_____	_____	_____
f. la poesía	_____	_____	_____
g. la música folklórica	_____	_____	_____
h. el regateo	_____	_____	_____
i. las bromas	_____	_____	_____
j. las maldiciones	_____	_____	_____
k. el hablar con niños	_____	_____	_____
l. el mentir	_____	_____	_____
m. el persuadir	_____	_____	_____

27. Para cada par de características, marque con una X en la escala cómo se siente Ud. hacia el **español**.

Bonito	___	___	___	___	___	Feo
Rico	___	___	___	___	___	Pobre
Ruidoso	___	___	___	___	___	Musical
Preciso	___	___	___	___	___	Vago
Ilógico	___	___	___	___	___	Lógico
Sencillo	___	___	___	___	___	Sofisticado
Rítmico	___	___	___	___	___	Irregular
Refinado	___	___	___	___	___	Vulgar
Sin color	___	___	___	___	___	Colorido
Privado	___	___	___	___	___	Público
Superior	___	___	___	___	___	Inferior
No puro	___	___	___	___	___	Puro
Tranquilo	___	___	___	___	___	Nervioso
Agil	___	___	___	___	___	Torpe
Común	___	___	___	___	___	Sagrado

Gracias por su participación

List of Modifications Made to Questionnaires

Item on HSD Questionnaire	Modification made to HSS Questionnaire
(3.) If not born in the United States, how old were you when you came? _____	4. Age of Arrival to U.S.
4. Last grade you completed F S J Sr	Eliminated
5. Year you dropped out: 19____	Eliminated
6. What was the main reason you dropped out?	Eliminated
7. What other factors influenced your decision?	Eliminated
8. Who did you discuss your decision to drop out with?_____	Eliminated
9. Did your best friend in high school agree with this decision? Y N Don't know	Eliminated
10. Have you considered returning for your high school diploma or GED? Y N	Eliminated
13. Please answer the following questions using section A or B (as indicated) from the answer sheet.	Please answer the following questions by circling the options provided [Spanish, English Both] or [Excellent, Well, Fair, Poor]
14. Please fill in the following chart about your family members and friendswith whom you speak frequently. Please mention if they are male or female relatives and use sections C and D from the answer sheet where shown.	...and use sections A and B from the answer sheet where shown.
17. At your permanent address, who is the head of your house?_____	Eliminated
22a-k (worded in past tense)	Changed to present tense
22b. What grades did you usually get ? (Use Section E from the answer sheet)	[Options provided: A's, A's&B's, B's, B's&C's, C's, C's&D's, D's, D's&F's, F's]
22c.(Use Section f)	[Options provided: Y N]
22e. Were you ever in serious trouble with the law? Y N	Eliminated

23. When you were in high school, how much did your parents...(Use section F)	Changed to present tense; [Options provided: Often, Sometimes, Never]
23a. ...speak with teachers or other school officials?	Eliminated
23d. ...take you to museums or other cultural events?	Eliminated
24. Answer the following questions about your best friend during high school.	Eliminated
24a. Did he/she ever cut class? (Use Section F)	Eliminated
24b. Was he/she ever suspended or put on probation? Y N	Eliminated
24c. Was he/she ever in serious trouble with the law? Y N	Eliminated
24d. Did he/she ever participate in any extracurricular activities offered by your school (sports, clubs)? Y N	Eliminated
24e. Was he/she popular in school? Y N	Eliminated
24f. Is he/she still your best friend now?YN	Eliminated
24g. Did he/she finish high school? Y N	Eliminated
24h. What sex is your best friend?	Eliminated
24i. What is your best friend doing now?	Eliminated
25. When you were in high school, how important was the following to you? (Use section G)	Eliminated
25a. finding a steady job	Eliminated
25b. having close friends	Eliminated
25c. Having lots of money	Eliminated
25d. Living close to parents	Eliminated
25e. Moving to a different area	Eliminated

26. When you were in high school, how much of your free time did you spend...(Use section F)	Changed to present tense.
26c. thinking and daydreaming alone?	Eliminated
26d. reading for pleasure? (F)	Eliminated
26e. with your family ? (F)	Eliminated
27. Did you have a job when you were in high school? Y N If yes,	Eliminated
27a. ...did you find that working was more enjoyable than going to school? Y N	Eliminated
27b. ...did you feel that working was more important than going to school?Y N	Eliminated
27c. ... please fill in the following information.	Eliminated
During what grades did you work?	Eliminated
For how long?	Eliminated
How many hours per week?	Eliminated
Did you speak Spanish regularly to your... ... boss? ...coworkers? ...customers?	Eliminated
28. What language do you use most often when you...(Use section C)	[Options provided: Spanish, English, Both]
29. What language do you use when you...(Use section C)	...use most often when you...[Options provided: Spanish, English, Both]
30. What language do you use when the person you're speaking to is bilingual...(Use section C)	Options provided [Spanish Only, Mixed Sp/Eng, English Only, Either Sp or Eng]

31. How likely are you to become <u>close</u> friends with: (Use section H)	Eliminated
31a. Latinos who speak only Spanish	Eliminated
31b. Latinos who speak only English	Eliminated
31c. Latinos who are bilingual	Eliminated
31e. Non-Latinos who speak only English	Eliminated
31f. Non-Latinos who are Spanish/ English bilinguals	Eliminated
32. The following statements refer to **Spanish**. Please use answers choices from section I.	...**Spanish**. Please say if you **A**gree, **D**isagree or are **U**ndecided. [Options provided: A, D, U]
33. The following questions refer to **English**. Please use answers choices from section I.	..**English**. Please say if you **A**gree, **D**isagree or are **U**ndecided. [Options provided: A, D, U]
34. Using the choices in section A, say which language(s) is (are) most appropriate for the following situations.	Please mark which language or language(s) is (are) most appropriate for the following situations [Options provided: Spanish, English, Either]
35. For each pair of characteristics, please say the number on the scale that represents how you feel about the **Spanish** language.	For each pair of characteristics, place an X on the line that represents how you feel about the **Spanish** language. [Five lines provided in place of numbers.]

<u>Items not on HSD Questionnaire Added to HSS Questionnaire</u>

6. What year are you in school? _____

(7.) How many hours do you work per week? _____

8. What is the highest academic degree you plan to work to achieve in your lifetime? (Circle one choice) [Options provided: GED, High school diploma, Vocational school degree, Junior college degree (2 years) Bachelor's degree (4 years), Graduate/Professional degree, None of the above]

9. After obtaining your highest degree, what do you intend to have as a profession? _____

Spanish Vocabulary List (Proficiency Measure)

<u>Changes made to HSS Questionnaire items to make CS Questionnaire</u>

Modified: 6a. What year are you in college?

Added: 6b. Current major _____   Current GPA _____/5.0

Added:18. What high school(s) did you attend and where? _____   _____
                                                                        school(s)   city

Modified: 18b-j (changed to past tense)

Modified: 21 When you have access to media in both Spanish and English, what language do you use most often when you...

Spanish Vocabulary Test

Nombre_____   Número _____

Edad_____   Sexo: Hombre   Mujer

¿Dónde nació?_____ ¿Cuánto tiempo lleva en los EEUU?_____

¿Cuál fue el último grado de escuela que Ud. terminó?_____

¿Cuál fue el primer idioma que Ud. aprendió a...

    ...hablar?_____   ...leer?_____   ...escribir?_____

Ud. cree que...

habla español	excelente	bien	regular	mal
entiende español	excelente	bien	regular	mal
lee español	excelente	bien	regular	mal
escribe español	excelente	bien	regular	mal

Ud. cree que...

habla inglés	excelente	bien	regular	mal
entiende inglés	excelente	bien	regular	mal
lee inglés	excelente	bien	regular	mal
escribe inglés	excelente	bien	regular	mal

En las siguentes hojas hay una lista de palabras en español. Para cada palabra marque una X en la columna que corresponde a *su opinión* sobre la frecuencia que se oye o se usa esa palabra en conversaciones cotidianas. Favor de poner un círculo alrededor de cualquier palabra que no conoce. Las categorías se definen de la siguiente manera:

Muy común: se oye o se usa con una alta frecuencia (p. ej.: casa)

    Común: se oye o se usa a menudo pero no tanto como una palabra
                    en la categoría "muy común" (p. ej.: maleta)

    Rara vez: se oye o se usa de vez en cuando, pero menos que una
                    palabra en la categoría "común" (p. ej.: sapo)

    Muy rara: se oye o se usa muy poco   (p. ej.: asesor)

Modelo para marcar respuestas:

	Muy común	Común	Rara	Muy rara
casa	_X_	___	___	___

Gracias por su participación.

	Muy común	común	Rara vez	Muy rara		Muy común	común	Rara vez	Muy rara
acatar	___	___	___	___	exigir	___	___	___	___
acertar	___	___	___	___	éxito	___	___	___	___
ahogarse	___	___	___	___	fracasar	___	___	___	___
alabar	___	___	___	___	galardón	___	___	___	___
alcalde	___	___	___	___	grapas (unas)	___	___	___	___
alcancía	___	___	___	___	gripe	___	___	___	___
alcanzar	___	___	___	___	guerra	___	___	___	___
aliento	___	___	___	___	herida (una)	___	___	___	___
alma	___	___	___	___	hermano	___	___	___	___
aprender	___	___	___	___	hincar	___	___	___	___
asunto	___	___	___	___	hogar	___	___	___	___
aula	___	___	___	___	huelga	___	___	___	___
beca	___	___	___	___	huésped	___	___	___	___
canicas	___	___	___	___	iglesia	___	___	___	___
caudillo	___	___	___	___	joven (un)	___	___	___	___
chismear	___	___	___	___	juguete	___	___	___	___
cicatriz	___	___	___	___	junta	___	___	___	___
cita	___	___	___	___	lápida	___	___	___	___
conocimiento	___	___	___	___	lápiz	___	___	___	___
conseguir	___	___	___	___	limosna	___	___	___	___
consentir	___	___	___	___	llorar	___	___	___	___
costra	___	___	___	___	madre	___	___	___	___
creencia	___	___	___	___	manda (una)	___	___	___	___
cuaresma	___	___	___	___	marear	___	___	___	___
derecho (un)	___	___	___	___	marido	___	___	___	___
desfile	___	___	___	___	mecer	___	___	___	___
desmayarse	___	___	___	___	merecer	___	___	___	___
desmentir	___	___	___	___	meta	___	___	___	___
dibujo	___	___	___	___	mollera	___	___	___	___
dulce	___	___	___	___	moño	___	___	___	___
empate	___	___	___	___	muestra (una)	___	___	___	___
engañar	___	___	___	___	muletas	___	___	___	___
estafa	___	___	___	___	nieto	___	___	___	___
estante	___	___	___	___	orgullo	___	___	___	___

	Muy común	común	Rara vez	Muy rara		Muy común	común	Rara vez	Muy rara
pañal	—	—	—	—	ronchas	—	—	—	—
pancarta	—	—	—	—	sacerdote	—	—	—	—
pareja	—	—	—	—	salud	—	—	—	—
payaso	—	—	—	—	santiguar	—	—	—	—
pecar	—	—	—	—	sonaja	—	—	—	—
pedir	—	—	—	—	sondeo	—	—	—	—
perder	—	—	—	—	suegro	—	—	—	—
pila	—	—	—	—	sueño (un)	—	—	—	—
pizarra	—	—	—	—	suerte	—	—	—	—
porvenir	—	—	—	—	tablero	—	—	—	—
pregunta	—	—	—	—	tarea	—	—	—	—
prole	—	—	—	—	temer	—	—	—	—
punto	—	—	—	—	ternura	—	—	—	—
pupitre	—	—	—	—	tijeras	—	—	—	—
querer	—	—	—	—	títere	—	—	—	—
regalo (un)	—	—	—	—	trabajo	—	—	—	—
regañar	—	—	—	—	verruga	—	—	—	—
rezar	—	—	—	—	yerno	—	—	—	—

Word Frequencies for Spanish Vocabulary Test

Category	Word	Average		Category	Word	Average
Politics	desmentir	3.8667		School	lápiz	3.9333
Politics	perder	3.5333		School	dibujo	3.6667
Politics	derecho (un)	3.2667		School	pregunta	3.6667
Politics	engañar	3.1333		School	tijeras	3.6667
Politics	guerra	3.0667		School	aprender	3.6
Politics	asunto	3		School	tarea	3.6
Politics	junta	2.9333		School	conocimiento	3.5333
Politics	desfile	2.8		School	grapas	2.8667
Politics	alcalde	2.6667		School	beca	2.6667
Politics	empate	2.5333		School	exigir	2.6
Politics	huelga	2.3333		School	tablero	2.4
Politics	estafa	2.1333		School	pizarra	2.1333
Politics	pancarta	1.6		School	aula	1.8
Politics	sondeo	1.3333		School	estante	1.6667
Politics	caudillo	1.1333		School	pupitre	1.1333
Religion	iglesia	4		Medical	salud	3.9333
Religion	pedir	3.6667		Medical	punto	3.6
Religion	pila	3.3333		Medical	herida	3.4
Religion	rezar	3.3333		Medical	desmayarse	3.1333
Religion	manda	3.1333		Medical	muestra	3.1333
Religion	alma	2.9333		Medical	ahogarse	3.0667
Religion	pecar	2.9333		Medical	cita	3.0667
Religion	hincar	2.8667		Medical	gripe	3
Religion	limosna	2.8		Medical	marear	2.8
Religion	sacerdote	2.7333		Medical	ronchas	2.6
Religion	creencia	2.6		Medical	muletas	2.3333
Religion	alabar	2.4667		Medical	cicatriz	2.0667
Religion	cuaresma	2.1333		Medical	costra	1.8667
Religion	lápida	1.5333		Medical	mollera	1.7333
Religion	santiguar	1.5333		Medical	verruga	1.7333
Family	hermano	3.9333		Childhood	joven	3.9333
Family	madre	3.9333		Childhood	juguete	3.9333
Family	marido	3.9333		Childhood	llorar	3.8667
Family	pareja	3.9333		Childhood	dulce	3.8
Family	nieto	3.8667		Childhood	payaso	3.6
Family	regañar	3.6		Childhood	regalo	3.5333
Family	suegro	3.5333		Childhood	moño	3.2667
Family	yerno	3.4		Childhood	consentir	3
Family	querer	3.3333		Childhood	pañal	2.7333
Family	hogar	3.2667		Childhood	temer	2.7333

Family	chismear	2.9333
Family	ternura	2.6667
Family	huésped	2.0667
Family	acatar	1.9333
Family	prole	1

Category	Word	Average
Dreams	trabajo	4
Dreams	sueño	3.9333
Dreams	alcanzar	3.7333
Dreams	suerte	3.5333
Dreams	conseguir	3.2
Dreams	éxito	3.2
Dreams	merecer	3
Dreams	aliento	2.9333
Dreams	orgullo	2.8
Dreams	porvenir	2.8
Dreams	fracasar	2.6667
Dreams	meta	2.3333
Dreams	acertar	2.2
Dreams	galardón	1.5333

Childhood	alcancía	2.4
Childhood	canicas	2.2
Childhood	mecer	2.2
Childhood	sonaja	1.8667
Childhood	titere	1.8667

Spanish Vocabulary List

Listen to the tape recording as it pronounces the words in Spanish from the first column. Circle the English translation that you think is the closest to the meaning of the Spanish word. Not all of the Spanish words listed are real, so if you have never heard the word before, or don't know its meaning , circle "Not a word".

Escuche la grabación para la pronunciación de las palabras españolas de la primera columna. Haga un círculo a la traducción en inglés que Ud. considera que es la más cercana a su significado. No todas las palabras españolas son verdaderas, entonces si no conoce una palabra, o si no sabe su significado, haga un círculo a la frase "Not a word".

Examples (Ejemplos):

CASA	suitcase	box	house	Not a word
COMER	to sleep	to eat	to talk	Not a word

SPANISH	English Translations			
1. ACATAR	to pay attention to	to be caught	to disobey	Not a word
2. ACERTAR	to mess up	to act	to get right	Not a word
3. ADULIJIR	to overcome problems	to polish	to follow your dream	Not a word
4. ALCALDE	soup	mayor	senator	Not a word
5. ALCANCIA	toy horn	piggy bank	sewer	Not a word
6. ALCANZAR	to give up	to reach	to heat up	Not a word
7. APRENDER	to arrest	to teach	to learn	Not a word
8. CAUDILLO	ballot box	gravy	leader	Not a word
9. CHISMEAR	to gossip	to comfort	to spark	Not a word
10. CILONQUE	water tower	floor wax	bucket	Not a word
11. COSTRA	oyster	stitch	scab	Not a word
12. DESMAYARSE	to breathe	to faint	to be sad	Not a word
13. DESMENTIR	to deny	to qualify	to run for office	Not a word
14. DESMOLAR	to not play fair	to make a mistake	to break something	Not a word
15. DIBUJO	drawing	owl	crayon	Not a word
16. ESTANTE	bus stop	desk lamp	bookcase	Not a word
17. EXIGIR	to demonstrate	to demand	to go away	Not a word
18. EXITO	exit	dream	success	Not a word
19. FRACASAR	to work for	to fail	to fry in oil	Not a word
20. GALARDON	reward	head of family	rejection	Not a word
21. GOVINO	ghost	sacred wine	sparrow	Not a word
22. GRAPAS	rulers	grapes	staples	Not a word
23. GUERRA	wool cap	protest	war	Not a word
24. HUELGA	union	strike	hole	Not a word
25. HUESPED	guest	pillowcase	host	Not a word

SPANISH	English Translations			
26. IGLESIA	igloo	church	altar	Not a word
27. LAPIDA	graveyard	tombstone	liquid	Not a word
28. LEGONAR	to complain	to recite poetry	to punish	Not a word
29. LIMOSNA	limousine	hymn	donation	Not a word
30. LLORAR	to laugh	to call to someone	to cry	Not a word
31. MAREAR	to feel dizzy	to sail	to feel sleepy	Not a word
32. MUELARA	kneecap	blister	grinding stone	Not a word
33. MULETAS	ponies	crutches	plaster casts	Not a word
34. ORGULLO	pride	persistence	gorilla	Not a word
35. PAREJA	wedding ring	bird	couple	Not a word
36. PAYASO	clown	birthday cake	string	Not a word
37. PECAR	to sin	to snack	to bury	Not a word
38. PUPITRE	butterfly	school desk	pencil sharpener	Not a word
39. RECIQUE	cotton candy	circus tent	water pump	Not a word
40. REGANAR	to refund money	to respect	to scold	Not a word
41. REZAR	to share	to shave	to pray	Not a word
42. SALUD	blood	health	salad	Not a word
43. SANTIGUAR	to bleed	to confess	to bless	Not a word
44. SONAJA	baby rattle	toy soldier	school bell	Not a word
45. SONDEO	opinion poll	campaign rally	stereo	Not a word
46. SUBCOLAR	to move around	to work in a group	to assign a task	Not a word
47. TEMER	to calm	to take away	to fear	Not a word
48. TERNURA	veal	affection	laughter	Not a word
49. TITERE	giant	puppet	kite	Not a word
50. VERRUGA	wart	freckle	turtle	Not a word

Bibliography

Adorno, W. 1973. The attitudes of selected Mexican and Mexican American parents in regards to bilingual/bicultural education. Unpublished doctoral dissertation, United States International University.

Agheyisi, Rebecca, and Joshua A. Fishman. 1970. Language Attitude Studies: A Brief Survey of Methodological Approaches. *Anthropological Linguistics* 12 (5):137-157.

Aguirre, Adalberto. 1982. Language use patterns of adolescent Chicanos in a California border town. In *Bilingualism and language contact*, edited by F. Barkin, E. Brandt and J. Ornstein. New York: Teachers College, Columbia University, pp. 278-289.

Aguirre, Adalberto. 1984. Language use in bilingual Mexican-American households. *Social Science Quarterly* 65:565-571.

Amastae, Jon and Lucía Elías-Olivares. 1978. Attitudes toward varieties of Spanish. In M. Paradis (Ed.), *The fourth LACUS forum,* Columbia, S.C.: Hornbeam Press, Inc., pp. 286-302.

Attinasi, John J. 1985. Hispanic Attitudes in Northwest Indiana and New York. In *Spanish language use and public life in the United States*, edited by L. Elias-Olivares, E. A. Leone, R. Cisneros and J. Gutierrez. Berlin: Walter de Gruyter & Co., pp. 27-58.

Ayer, George W. 1971. Language and attitudes of the Spanish-speaking youth of the Southwestern United States. In *Applications of Linguistics*, edited by G. E. P. J. Trim. Cambridge: Cambridge University Press, pp. 115-120.

Bachman, Jerald G., Swayzer Green, and Iliona D. Wirtanen. 1971. *Youth in Transition: Dropping out-Problem or symptom?* Vol. 3. Ann Arbor: University of Michigan, Institute of Social Research.

Bachman, Jerald G., P. M. O'Malley, and J. Johnson. 1971. *Youth in transition: Adolescence to adulthood—Change and stability in the lives of young men.* Vol. 6. Ann Arbor: University of Michigan, Institute for Social Research.

Bachman, Lyle and A. Palmer. 1989. The construct validation of self-ratings of communicative language ability. *Language Testing* 6 (1):14-25.

Barker, George C. 1972. *Social Functions of Language in a Mexican-American Community.* Vol. 22, *Anthropological Papers of the University of Arizona.* Tucson, AZ: University of Arizona Press.

Barro, Stephen M. 1984. *The incidence of dropping out: A descriptive analysis.* Washington, D. C.: SMB Economic Research, Inc.

Cardoza, Desdemona. 1982. The effect of the bilingual education experience on the language attitudes of Spanish/English bilingual children. Doctoral dissertation, Psychology, University of California, Riverside, Riverside.

Carranza, Miguel. 1982. Attitudinal Research on Hispanic Language Varieties. In *Attitudes towards Language Variation: Social and Applied Contexts,* edited by E. B. Ryan and H. Giles. London: Edward Arnold, pp. 63-83.

Carranza, Michael A., and Ellen Bouchard Ryan. 1975. Evaluative Reactions of Bilingual Anglo and Mexican American Adolescents Toward Speakers of English and Spanish. *International Journal of the Sociology of Language* 6 (Language Attitudes II):83-104.

Census of Population and Housing, 1990. 1993. *1990 Census of population and housing: Summary tape file 3C.* Washington, D. C.: U. S. Department of Commerce, Bureau of the Census. Computer laser optical disks.

Chapa, Jorge, and Richard R. Valencia. 1993. Latino population growth, demographic characteristics, and educational stagnation: An examination of recent trends. *Hispanic Journal of Behavioral Sciences* 15 (2):165-187.

Chicago, The City of. 1991. School Report Card: Benito Juárez High School. Chicago, Illinois: School District 299.

Chicago, City of. 1991. School Report Card: Farragut High School. Chicago, Illinois: School District 299.

Chicago, City of. 1991. School Report Card: Kelly High School. Chicago, Illinois: School District 299.

Chicago, The City of. 1991. School Report Card: Kelvyn High School. Chicago, Illinois: School District 299.

Chicago, The City of. 1991. School Report Card: Lakeview High School. Chicago, Illinois: School District 299.

Chicago, The City of. 1991. School Report Card: Roberto Clemente High School. Chicago: School District 299.

Chicago, The City of. 1991. School Report Card: Schurz High School. Chicago: School District 299.

Chicago, The City of. 1991. School Report Card: Wells High School. Chicago, Illinois: School District 299.

Cisneros, Rene, and Elizabeth. A. Leone. 1983. Mexican American language communities in the Twin Cities: An example of contact and recontact. In *Spanish in the U. S. setting: Beyond the Southwest*, edited by L. Elias-Olivares. Rosslyn, Virginia: National Clearinghouse for Bilingual Education, pp. 181-210.

Cohen, Andrew D. 1974. Mexican-American Evaluation Judgements About Language Varieties. *International Journal of the Sociology of Language* 3 (Language Attitudes I):33-51.

Cooper, Robert L., and Joshua A. Fishman. 1974. The Study of Language Attitudes. *International Journal of the Sociology of Language* 3 (Language Attitudes I):5-19.

Cooper, Robert L., and Joshua A. Fishman. 1977. A Study of Language Attitudes. In *The Spread of English*, edited by J. A. Fishman, R. L. Cooper and A. W. Conrad. Rowley, Massachusetts: Newbury House Publishers, Inc, pp. 239-276.

Cuban, L. 1989. Panel discussion and concluding remarks. In *What do anthropologists have to say about dropouts: The first centennial conference on children at risk* edited by H.T. Trueba, G. Spindler & L. Spindler. London: Falmer Press, pp. 125-152.

Cummins, James. 1979. Linguistic interdependence and the educational development of bilingual children. *Review of Educational Research 49*, 222-251.

Cummins, James. 1989. Language and literacy acquisition in bilingual contexts. *Journal of Multilingual and Multicultural Development 10*(1), 17-31.

Curiel, Herman, James A. Rosenthal, and Herbert G. Richek. 1986. Impacts of bilingual education of secondary school grades, attendance, retentions, and drop-out. *Hispanic Journal of Behavioral Sciences* 8 (4):357-367.

Davis, Cary B., Carl Haub, and JoAnne Willette. 1983. U.S. Hispanics: Changing the face of America. *Population Bulletin, 38* (3): 1-43.

D'Amico, R. 1984. Does employment during high school impair academic progress? *Sociology of Education* 57:152-164.

De Avila, Edward A. and Sharon Duncan. 1985. The Language-Minority Child: A Psychological, Linguistic, and Social Analysis. In Susan F. Chipman, Judith W. Segal and Robert Glaser, eds., *Thinking and Learning Skills: (Vol. 2: Research and Open Questions)*, pp. 245–274. Hillsdale, NJ: Lawrence Erlbaum Associates.

Diaz, R. 1983. Thought and two languages: The impact of bilingualism on cognitive development. *Review of Educational Research, 10:*23-54.

Dornic, Stanislav. 1978. The bilingual's performance: language dominance, stress and individual differences. In D. Gerver and H. Sinaiko (eds.) *Language interpretation and communication.* New York: Plenum Press.

Durán, Richard P. 1983. *Hispanics' education and background: Predictors of college achievement.* New York: College Entrance Examination Board.

Ekstrom, R. B., M. E. Goerts, J. M. Pollack, and Rock. D. A. 1987. Who drops out of high school and why? Findings from a national study. In *School dropouts: patterns and policies*, edited by G. Natriello. New York: Columbia University Teachers College Press, pp. 52-69.

Elías-Olivares, Lucía. 1976a. Chicano language varieties and uses in East Austin. In *SWALLOW IV: Linguistics and Education*, edited by M. R. Mazon. San Diego: Institute for Cultural Pluralism, pp. 195-220.

Elías-Olivares, Lucía. 1976b. Language use in a Chicano community: A sociolinguistic approach. *Working Papers in Sociolinguistics 30.* Austin: Southwest Educational Development Laboratory.

Elías-Olivares, Lucía, ed. 1983. *Spanish in the U.S. setting: Beyond the Southwest.* Rosslyn, Virginia: National Clearinghouse for Bilingual Education.

Elías-Olivares, Lucía. 1995. Discourse strategies of Mexican American Spanish. In *Spanish in four continents: studies in language contact and bilingualism*, edited by C. Silva-Corvalán. Washington, D. C.: Georgetown University Press, pp. 227-240.

Farr, Marcia, and Juan C. Guerra. 1995. Literacy in the community: A study of Mexicano families in Chicago. *Discourse Processes* 19:7-19.

Fishman, Joshua A. 1973. The third century of non-English language maintenance and non-Anglo ethnic maintenance in the United States of America. *TESOL Quarterly 7*, 221-233.

Fishman, Joshua A. 1977. The Spread of English as a New Perspective for the Study of "Language Maintenance and Language Shift". In *The Spread of English*, edited by J. A. Fishman, R. L. Cooper and A. W. Conrad. Rowley, Massachusetts: Newbury House Publishers, Inc., pp.108-133.

Fishman, Joshua A., Robert L. Cooper, and Roxanna Ma. 1971. *Bilingualism in the barrio, Indiana University Publications, Language Science Monographs.* The Hague, The Netherlands: Mouton & Co.

Fishman, Joshua A., V. Nahirny, J. Hoffman, and R. Hayden. 1966. *Language loyalty in the United States.* The Hague: Mouton.

Floyd, Mary Beth. 1985. Spanish in the Southwest: Language Maintenance or Shift? In *Spanish language use and public life in the United States*, edited by L. Elias-Olivares. Berlin: Walter de Gruyter & Co., pp. 13-26.

Ford Foundation. 1984. *Los Hispanos: Problemas y oportunidades* (Documento de trabajo de la Fundación Ford). New York: Ford Foundation.

Galindo, D. Letticia. 1991. A sociolinguistic study of Spanish language maintenance and language shift towards English among Chicanos. *Lenguas Modernas* 18:107-116.

Galván, José L., James A. Pierce, and Gary N. Underwood. 1976. Relationships between teacher attitudes and differences in the English of bilinguals. In *Swallow IV: Linguistics and education*, edited by M. R. Mazon. San Diego, CA: Institute for Cultural Pluralism, School of Education, San Diego State University, pp. 279-314.

García, Ofelia, Isabel Evangelista, Mabel Martínez, Carmen Disla, and Paulino Bonifacio. 1988. Spanish language use and attitudes: A study of two New York City communitities. *Language in Society* 17:475-511.

Giles, Howard, Angie Williams, Diane M. Mackie, and Francine Rosselli. 1995. Reactions to Anglo- and Hispanic-American accented speakers: Affect, identity, persuasion, and the English-only controversy. *Language and Communication* 15 (2):107-120.

Grebler, Leo, Jean W. Moore, and Ralph C. Guzman. 1970. *The Mexican American people: The nation's largest minority.* New York: The Free Press.

Griswold del Castillo, Richard. 1990. *The Treaty of Guadalupe Hidalgo: A legacy of conflict.* Norman, OK: University of Oklahoma Press.

Gynan, Shaw Nicholas. 1985. The Influence of Language Background on Attitudes Toward Native and Nonnative Spanish. *The Bilingual Review* XII (1 & 2):33-42.

Hakuta, Kenji. 1986. *Mirror of Language.* New York: Basic Books.

Hakuta, Kenji, and D. D'Andrea. 1992. Some properties of bilingual maintenance and loss in Mexican background high school students. *Applied Linguistics* 13 (1):72-99.

Hancin-Bhatt, Barbara, and William Nagy. 1994. Lexical transfer and second language morphological development. *Applied Psycholinguistics* 15:289-310.

Hannum, Thomasina. 1978. Attitudes of Bilingual Students Toward Spanish. *Hispania* 61 (March):90-94.

Hart-González, Lucinda, and Marcia Feingold. 1990. Retention of Spanish in the home. *International Journal of the Sociology of Language* 84:5-34.

Hauser, Robert M., and Hanam Samuel Phang. 1993. *Trends in high school dropout among white, black, and Hispanic youth, 1973 to 1989, Discussion Paper No. 1007-93.* Madison, Wisconsin: Institute for Research on Poverty, University of Wisconsin-Madison.

Hernández-Chávez, Eduardo, Andrew D. Cohen, and Anthony F. Beltramo, eds. 1975. *El lenguaje de los Chicanos: Regional and social characteristics used by Mexican Americans.* Arlington, VA: Center for Applied Linguistics.

Hirano-Nakanishi, Marsha. 1986. The extent and relevance of pre-high school attrition and delayed education for Hispanics. *Hispanic Journal of Behavioral Sciences* 8 (3):61-76.

Hirano-Nakanish, Marsha J., and R. Leticia Díaz. 1982. *Differential educational attainment among "at-risk" youth: A case study of language minority youth of Mexican descent and low socioeconomic status, ERIC Document Reproduction Service No. ED 241 832.* Los Alamitos, CA: National Center for Bilingual Research.

Hofman, John E., and Judith Cais. 1984. Children's attitudes to language maintenance and shift. *International Journal of the Sociology of Language* 50:147-153.

Huang, Gary G. 1992. *Self-reported biliteracy and self esteem: A study of Mexican American 8th graders, ERIC Reproduction Service No. ED 356 937.* Charleston, WV: Appalachia Educational Laboratory.

Hurtado, Aida, and P. Gurín. 1987. Ethnic identity and bilingualism attitudes. *Hispanic Journal of Behavioral Sciences* 9 (1):1-18.

Hutchinson, R. 1990. Language patterns among Hispanic groups in Chicago. (manuscript)

Kanellos, Nicolas, ed. 1993. *The Hispanic-American almanac: A reference work on Hispanics in the United States.* Detroit: Gale Research Inc.

Kyle, Charles L. 1989. Lost! An initial study of the magnitude and reasons for early school leavers from Chicago Public Schools. A report to Illinois Attorney General Neil F. Hartigan. ERIC Document Reproduction Service No. ED 309 220. Chicago, IL: Loyola University.

Kyle, Charles L., John Lane, Joyce A. Sween, and Armando Triana. 1986. We have a choice: Students at risk of leaving Chicago public schools. A report to the Chicago Board of Education and the Illinois Attorney General. ERIC Reproduction Service No. ED 273 710. Chicago, IL: Chicago Area Studies Center, Center for Research on Hispanics, De Paul University.

Kyle, Charles L., and Erica Sufritz. 1990. Invisible. Good schools = Healthy economy. Poor academic achievement = Increased unemployment. A longitudinal pilot study on the relationship between job growth and school performance in 15 of Illinois' largest counties. A report to Cook County Assessor Thomas Hymes. . ERIC Document Reproduction Service No. ED 318 816. Chicago, IL: Loyola University.

Laosa, L. M. 1975. Bilingualism in three United States Hispanic groups: Contextual use of language by children and adults in their families. *Journal of Educational Psychology* 67:617-627.

1994. Language woes affect Hispanic dropout rate. *The Champaign-Urbana News-Gazette*, September 14, 1994, D1.

LaTouche, Portia. 1976. English-Spanish bilingualism and bilingual attitudes. In *SWALLOW IV: Linguistics and education*, edited by M. R. Mazon. San Diego, CA: Institute for Cultural Pluralism, pp. 315-325.

Levin, H. 1972. The costs to the Nation of inadequate education (Report to the Select Committee on Equal Educational Opportunity, U. S. Senate). Washington, D. C.: Government Printing Office.

Lewin-Epstein, Noel. 1981. *Youth employment during high school. An analysis of high school and beyond (NCES-81-249), ERIC Document Reproduction Service No. ED 203 198.* Chicago, IL: National Opinion Research Center.

López, David E. 1978. Chicano language loyalty in an urban setting. *Sociology and Social Research* 62:267-278.

López, David E. 1982. *Language maintenance and shift in the United States today: The basic patterns and their social implications.* Vol. Vol. III: Hispanics and Portuguese. Los Alamitos, CA: National Center for Bilingual Research.

Macías, Reynaldo. F. (1993. Language and ethnic classification of language minorities: Chicano and Latino students in the 1990s. *Hispanic Journal of Behavioral Sciences* 15 (2):230-257.

McClure, Erica F. 1977. Aspects of code-switching in the discourse of bilingual Mexican-American children (Technical Report No. 44). Washington, D.C.: National Institute of Education, Department of Health, Education and Welfare. (ERIC Document Reproduction Service No. ED 150 877)

McConnell, Beverly B. 1983. Individualized Bilingual Instruction: A Validated Program Model Effective with Both Spanish and Asian Language Students. In *Theory, Technology, and Public Policy on Bilingual Education*, edited by R. V. Padilla. Rosslyn, Virginia: National Clearinghouse for Bilingual Education, pp. 138-148.

Mejías, Hugo A., and Pamela L. Anderson. 1988. Attitude toward use of Spanish on the South Texas Border. *Hispania* 71 (May):401-407.

Nielsen, F. & Fernández, R. M. 1981. *Hispanic students in American high schools: Background characteristics and achievement*. Washington, DC: National Center for Education Statistics.

Oakes, Jeannie. 1985. *Keeping track: How schools structure inequality*. New Haven, CT: Yale University Press.

O'Hare, W. P. (1992) America's minorities—The demographics of diversity. *Population Bulletin, 47*(4). Washington, DC: Population Reference Bureau, Inc.

O'Malley, James M. 1987. *Academic growth of high school age Hispanic students in the United States.* Washington, D. C.: InterAmerica Research Associates.

Ornstein, Jacob. 1970. Sociolinguistics and new perspectives in the study of southwest Spanish. In *Studies in language and linguistics 1969-1970*, edited by J. Ornstein and R. W. Ewton. El Paso, TX: Western Press, pp. 127-184.

Ortiz, Vilma. 1989. Language background and literacy among Hispanic young adults. *Social Problems* 36 (2):149-164.

Orum, L. S. 1985. *The education of Hispanics: Selected statistics, ERIC Document Reproduction Service No. ED 262 121.* Washington, D. C.: National Council of La Raza.

Osgood, Charles E. 1964. Semantic Differential Technique in the Comparative Study of Cultures. *American Anthropologist* 66 (No. 3, Part 2):171-200.

Pallas, A. M. 1984. The determinants of high school dropout. Unpublished doctoral dissertation, The Johns Hopkins University.

Pallas, A. M. 1987. *School Dropouts in the United States.* Washington, D.C.: Center for Educational Statistics, Office of Educational Research and Improvement, U.S. Department of Education.

Peal, Elizabeth, and Wallace E. Lambert. 1962. The relation of bilingualism to intelligence. *Psychological Monographs* 76 (7):1-23.

Peñalosa, Fernando. 1980. *Chicano sociolinguistics: A brief introduction.* Rowley, Mass.: Newbury House.

Peñalosa, Fernando. 1981. Some Issues in Chicano Sociolinguistics. . In *Latino Language and Communicative Behavior*, edited by R. P. Duran. Norwood, New Jersey: ABLEX, pp. 3-18.

Pérez, S. M. , and D. De La Rosa Salazar. 1993. Economic, labor force, and social implications of Latino educational and population trends. *Hispanic Journal of Behavioral Sciences* 15 (2):188-229.

Poplack, Shana. 1982. Sometimes I'll start a sentence in Spanish y termino en espanol: Toward a typology of code-switching. In *Spanish in the United States: Sociolinguistic aspects*, edited by J. Amastae and L. Elias-Olivares. Cambridge: Cambridge University Press, pp. 230-263.

Ramírez, Karen G. 1974. Socio-cultural aspects of the Chicano dialect. In *Southwest are linguistics*, edited by G. D. Bills. San Diego, CA: Institute for Cultural Pluralism, San Diego State University, pp. 7-84.

Reyes, O. & Jason, L.A. 1993. Pilot study examining factors associated with academic success for Hispanic high school students. *Journal of Youth and Adolescence, 22*, 57-71.

Rock, D.A., Ekstrom, R. B., Goertz, M. E., & Pollack, J. 1986. *Study of excellence in high school education: Longitudinal study, 1980-1982 final report.* Washington, D.C.: Educational Testing Service.

Rosenbaum, James E. 1976. *Making inequality: The hidden curriculum of high school tracking.* New York: Wiley

Rosenbaum, James E. 1980. Track misperceptions and frustrated college plans: An analysis of the effects of tracks and track perceptions in the National Longitudinal Survey. *Sociology of Education, 53,* 74-88.

Rumberger, Russell W. 1983. Dropping out of high school: The influence of race, sex, and family background. *American Educational Research Journal* 20 (2):199-220.

Ryan, Elizabeth Bouchard, and Michael A. Carranza. 1977. Ingroup and Outgroup Reactions to Mexican American Language Varieties. In *Language, Ethnicity and Intergroup Relations,* edited by H. Giles. New York: Academic Press, pp. 59-82.

Silva-Corvalán, Carmen. 1983. Code-shifting patterns in Chicano Spanish. In *Spanish in the U. S. setting: Beyond the Southwest,* edited by L. Elías-Olivares. Rosslyn, VA: National Clearinghouse for Bilingual Education, pp. 69-88

Skrabanek, R. L. 1970. Language maintenance among Mexican-Americans. *International Journal of Comparative Sociology, 11,* 272-282.

Skutnabb-Kangas, Tove, and Pertti Toukomaa. 1976. *Teaching migrant children's mother tongue and learning the language of the host country in the context of the socio-cultural situation of the migrant family.* Tampere: UNESCO.

Solé, Yolanda. 1976. Language attitudes towards Spanish among Mexican American college students. In *SWALLOW IV: Linguistics and education,* edited by M. R. Mazon. San Diego, CA: Institute for Cultural Pluralism, pp. 327-347.

Solé, Yolanda. 1985. Spanish/English mother-tongue claiming: the 1980 census data, a subsample, and their sociodemographic correlates. *Hispania,* 68, 283–297.

Solé, Yolanda. 1990. Bilingualism: Stable or transitional? The case of Spanish in the United States. *International Journal of the Sociology of Language, 84,* 35-80.

St. Clair, R. N. 1982. From social history to language attitudes. In *Attitudes towards language variation: Social and applied contexts*, edited by E. B. Ryan and H. Giles. London: Edward Arnold, pp. 164-174.

Steinberg, Laurence, Patricia Lin Blinde, and Kenyon S. Chan. 1984. Dropping out among language minority youth. *Review of Educational Research* 54 (1):113-132.

Steinberg, Laurence D., Ellen Greenberger, Laurie Garduque, and Sharon McAuliffe. 1982. High school students in the labor force: Some costs and benefits to schooling and learning. *Educational Evaluation and Policy Analysis* 4:363-372.

Suárez-Orozco, Marcelo M. 1987. Towards a psychosocial understanding of Hispanic adaptation to American schooling. In *Success or failure? Learning and language minority students*, edited by H. T. Trueba. Cambridge: Newbury House, pp. 156-168.

Teschner, Richard V., Garland Bills, D., and Jerry R. Craddock. 1975. *Spanish and English of United States Hispanos: A critical, annotated linguistic bibliography*. Arlington, VA: Center for Applied Linguistics.

Test of Adult Basic Education (TABE). (1994). Monterey, CA: CTB/Macmillan/McGraw-Hill.

Thompson, Roger M. 1974. Mexican American Language Loyalty and the Validity of the 1970 Census. *International Journal of the Sociology of Language* 2 (The American Southwest):7-18.

Trueba, Henry. T. 1989. *Raising silent voices: Educating the linguistic minorities for the 21st century*. New York: Newbury House.

U.S. Department of Education, National Center for Education Statistics. (1992a). *The condition of education: 1992*. Washington, D.C.: Author.

U.S. Department of Education, National Center for Education Statistics. (1992b). *Digest of educational statistics: 1992*. Washington, D.C.: Author.

United States Department of Education. (1992c). *A progress report to the Secretary of Education from the President's Advisory Commission on Educational Excellence for Hispanic Americans*. Washington, D. C.: Author.

U.S. Department of Education, National Center for Education Statistics. (1993). *Digest of educational statistics: 1993*. Washington, D.C.: Author.

U. S. House of Representatives. (1983). *The Hispanic population of the United States: An overview* (A report prepared by the Congressional Research Service for the Subcommittee on Census and Population of the Committee on Post Office and Civil Service, April 21, 1983). Washington, D.C.: U.S. Government Printing Office.

Usdansky, M. L. (1993, August 23) Report adds to debate on Hispanic progress. *USA Today*, pp. 1A, 6A.

Valdés, Guadalupe & Figueroa, Richard. A. (1994). *Bilingualism and Testing: A special case of bias.* Norwood, NJ: Ablex Publishing Corporation.

Valdivieso, Rafael. 1986. *Must they wait another generation? Hispanics and secondary school reform, ERIC Document Reproduction Service No. ED 273 705.* New York: Columbia University, Teachers College, ERIC Clearinghouse on Urban Education.

Valenzuela de la Garza, J., and Marcello Jr. Medina. 1985. Academic achievement as influenced by bilingual instruction for Spanish-dominant Mexican American children. *Hispanic Journal of Behavioral Sciences* 7 (3):247-259.

Valverde, Silvia A. 1986. *A comparative study of Hispanic LEP and non-LEP high school dropouts and Hispanic LEP and non-LEP high school graduates in an urban public school system in the southwestern United States.* Unpublished doctoral dissertation, University of Houston.

Vázquez, Marcherie. 1994. Escuelas latinas de Chicago todavía no pueden: Secundarias de Chicago debajo del promedio nacional. *!Exito! (Weekly publication of the Chicago Tribune)*, November 10, 1994, 7.

Vélez, W. 1989. High school attrition among Hispanic and non-Hispanic white youths. *Sociology of Education, 62*, 119-133.

Veltman, Calvin J. 1980. *Relative educational attainments of minority language children, 1976: A comparison to Black and White English language children.* Washington, D. C.: National Center for Education Statistics.

Veltman, Calvin J. 1983. *Language shift in the United States.* Vol. 34, *Contributions to the Sociology of Language.* Berlin: Walter de Gruyter & Co.

Veltman, C. J. 1988. *The future of the Spanish language in the U.S.* NY: Hispanic Policy Development Project.

Walker, C. L. 1987. Hispanic achievement: Old views and new perspectives. In *Success or failure? Learning and the language minority student*, edited by H. T. Trueba. Cambridge: Newbury House, pp. 15-32.

Watt, N. F., M. R. Guajardo, and H. J. Markham. 1987. *A psychological study of educational attainment among Hispanics (Final technical report on a research project sponsored by 2 + 2 Project), ERIC Document Reproduction Service No. ED 298 198.* Denver: Colorado State Department of Education.

Weinreich, Uriel. 1974. *Languages in contact: Findings and problems.* Mouton: The Hague.

Weller, G. 1983. The role of language as a cohesive force in the Hispanic speech community of Washington, D. C. In *Spanish in the U. S. setting: Beyond the Southwest*, edited by L. Elias-Olivares. Rosslyn, VA: National Clearinghouse for Bilingual Education, pp. 211-234.

Wentz, J., and Erica F. McClure. 1975. *Aspects of the syntax of the code-switched discourse of bilingual children, ERIC Document Reproduction Service No. ED 121 068.*

Wright, John W., ed. 1993. *The universal almanac 1993*. Kansas City: Andrews and McMeel.

Wright, John W., ed. 1995. *The universal almanac 1995*. Kansas City: Andrews and McMeel.

Zentella, Ana Celia. 1997. Latino youth at home, in their communities, and in school: The language link. *Education and Urban Society, 30:*122-130.

Index

Academic achievement
   academic profile, 52–59
   sociodemographic profile,
     46–51
   sociolinguistic profile, 59–76
Academic track. *See* Track
Adorno, W., 17, 163
Agheyisi, Rebecca, 16, 163
Aguirre, Adalberto, 23, 163
Amastae, Jon, 23, 163, 170
Attinasi, John J., 3, 16, 18, 22, 33,
   46, 163
Attitudes
   affective, x, 12, 17, 18, 33, 34,
     46, 71, 81, 86
   instrumental, x, 17, 18, 33, 34,
     46, 60, 72, 73, 76, 81, 86
   integrative, 17, 18, 33, 34, 46,
     72, 73, 74, 81, 88
   language loyalty, x, 17, 33, 34,
     46, 74, 75, 169
Ayer, George W., 17, 163

Bachman, Jerald G., 4, 5, 7, 8, 19,
   20, 163, 164
Barker, George C., 15, 164
Barro, Stephen M., 20, 164

Bilingual education, ix, 3, 11, 27,
   52, 53, 74, 87, 89, 164, 165

Cardoza, Desdemona, 164
Carranza, Miguel, 15, 17, 23, 33,
   164, 171
Census of Population and Hous-
   ing, 15, 164
Chapa, Jorge, xv, 9, 164
Chicago, xi, xiii, xiv, 9, 13, 15, 16,
   18, 26, 29, 30, 37, 52, 65,
   69, 82, 88, 164, 165, 166,
   168, 169, 173
Cisneros, Rene, 17, 163, 165
Codeswitching, 17, 22, 44, 66, 81,
   169, 170
Cohen, Andrew D., 22, 23, 165,
   167
Cooper, Robert L., 16, 17, 22, 32,
   33, 165, 166
Cuban, L., 5, 165
Cummins, James, 3, 11, 165
Curiel, Herman, 11, 165
Curriculum. *See* Track

D'Arnico, R., 20, 165
Davis, Cary, 165

De Avila, Edward, 3, 165
Díaz, R., 3, 165, 168
Disciplinary problems, ix, 8, 25,
    54, 55
Dornic, Stanislav, 33, 165
Dropout
    academic indicators, 7–9
    and attitudes toward school, 8
    consequences, xi–xii
    Hispanic profile, 4–13
    parents of, 9
    sociodemographic indicators,
        5–7
    and socioeconomic status, 6–7
    sociolinguistic indicators, 9–13
    and Spanish, xii–xiii
    and Spanish as "barrier,"
        xii–xiii
Durán, Richard P., 7, 10, 19, 21,
    52, 166

Ekstrom, R. B., xii, 4, 5, 7, 8, 9,
    19, 20, 25, 32, 51, 53, 54,
    56, 57, 58, 59, 83, 166,
    170
Elías-Olivares, Lucía, 12, 17, 18,
    22, 23, 32, 72, 163, 165,
    166, 170, 173
Employment, 6, 49, 51, 57, 76
English
    proficiency, ix, 3, 10, 28, 45,
        60, 61, 62, 63
    use of, 81, 88
Extracurricular activities, ix, 8, 27,
    32, 56, 57, 59, 76, 82

Farr, Marcia, 18, 166
First language, ix, 27, 45, 60, 61
Fishman, Joshua A., 14, 16, 17, 22,
    32, 33, 163, 165, 166
Floyd, Mary Beth, 16, 22, 166
Ford Foundation, 13, 166

Galindo, D. Letticia, 3, 12, 14, 15,
    16, 17, 22, 23, 72, 167
Galván, José L., 33, 167
García, Ofelia, 22, 32, 167
Giles, Howard, 23, 164, 167, 171
Grade point average, 4, 7, 8, 11,
    20, 27, 32, 36, 53, 54, 59,
    76, 82, 83, 84
Grade retention, 7, 10, 52, 82, 83,
    84
Grebler, Leo, 18, 167
Griswold del Castillo, Richard, 13,
    167
Gynan, Shaw Nicholas, 23, 167

Hakuta, Kenji, 3, 12, 22, 33, 36,
    167
Hancin-Bhatt, Barbara, 37, 167
Hannum, Thomasina, 17, 167
Hart-González, Lucinda, 23, 167
Hauser, Robert M., 5, 20, 21, 167
Hernández-Chávez, Eduardo, 22,
    23, 167
High School and Beyond, 4, 6, 8,
    19, 32
Hirano-Nakanishi, Marsha, 3, 4, 6,
    7, 11, 19, 168
Hispanic
    and poverty, 5–6
    dropout rate, xi
    English speaking, 11
    family profile, 5, 20, 26, 48, 51,
        76, 84
    Spanish speaking, 11
    youth and work, 6
Hofman, John E., 168
Huang, Gary G., 3, 168
Hurtado, Aida, 12, 47, 72, 168
Hutchinson, R., 18, 168

Identity, 12, 17, 31, 47, 51, 76,
    167, 168

Immigrant, 5, 9, 13, 14, 18, 26, 47, 79, 82

Kanelios, Nicolas, 13, 19, 168
Kyle, Charles L., xii, 9, 54, 168

Language appropriateness, 33, 67
Language attitudes, xiv, 4, 13, 16, 18, 23, 27, 28, 32, 34, 36, 46, 63, 76, 77, 81, 89, 164, 171
Language minority. *See* Linguistic minority
Language use, 4, 13, 15, 16, 18, 19, 22, 27, 28, 32, 33, 35, 36, 46, 59, 60, 63, 64, 65, 69, 70, 77, 80, 81, 89, 163, 166, 187
    generational, 16, 32, 46, 64, 65, 69, 77, 80
    interpersonal, 32, 33, 43, 45, 63, 64, 65, 66, 77, 78, 80, 85
    personal, 45, 66, 69, 77, 80
Language woes, 11, 168
Laosa, L. M., 16, 168
LaTouche, Portia, 17, 169
Levin, H., xii, 169
Lewin-Epstein, Noel, 6, 169
Linguistic minority, xii, 10, 11, 13, 17, 21, 22, 26, 79, 172
Literacy, 12, 18, 27, 37, 60, 62, 77, 85, 86, 88, 165, 170
López, David E., 12, 14, 17, 22, 169
Low English Proficient, 10, 21, 173

Macías, Reynaldo F., xiii, 169
McClure, Erica F., 22, 169, 173
McConnell, Beverly B., 169
Mejías, Hugo A., 169

Mexican, xii, xiii, xiv, 16, 3, 4, 8, 11, 12, 13, 14, 15, 16, 17, 18, 19, 22, 23, 25, 26, 27, 28, 29, 30, 31, 43, 45, 46, 47, 48, 59, 60, 63, 64, 70, 75, 76, 77, 78, 79, 80, 81, 82, 83, 84, 85, 87, 88, 89, 163, 164, 165, 166, 167, 168, 169, 171, 172, 173
    historical presence in U.S., 13–14
    Midwest population, 15

Nielsen, F., 10, 12, 169

Oakes, Jeannie, 21, 169
O'Hare, W. P., xi, xv, 14, 15, 16, 20, 169
O'Malley, James M., 4, 5, 8, 19, 20, 83, 164, 169
Ornstein, Jacob, 22, 23, 163, 170
Ortiz, Vilma, 12, 170
Orum, L. S., 7, 170
Osgood, Charles E., 33, 170
Overage phenomenon, 7

Pallas, A. M., xi, xii, 7, 20, 170
Parental education, 25, 49, 84
Parental occupations, 48
Parental support, ix, 27, 32, 58, 59, 83
Peal, Elizabeth, 170
Peñalosa, Fernando, 22, 23, 170
Pérez, S. M., xi, 170
Poplack, Shana, 22, 170

Ramírez, Karen G., 17, 170
Reyes, O., 9, 170
Rock, D. A., 4, 5, 19, 166, 170
Rosenbaum, James E., 21, 171
Rumberger, Russell W., xii, 7, 8, 9, 20, 57, 171

Ryan, Elizabeth Bouchard, 15, 17, 23, 33, 164, 171

Self-esteem, ix, 3, 8, 12, 27, 57, 58
Semantic differential, x, 33, 35, 70, 170
Sibling education, 50, 51, 76, 84
Silva-Corvalán, Carmen, 22, 166, 171
Skrabanek, R. L., 16, 171
Skutnabb-Kangas, Tove, 3, 11, 171
Socioeconomic status, 4, 5, 6, 7, 19, 25, 26, 47, 168
Solé, Yolanda, xii, 14, 15, 16, 17, 23, 33, 45, 47, 79, 171
Spanish
    maintenance of, xii, 17, 18, 25, 46, 77
    proficiency, ix, xiii, 4, 12, 28, 43, 45, 61, 62, 63, 80
    use of, xiv, 3, 12, 14, 15, 16, 18, 19, 22, 26, 35, 36, 46, 64, 65, 66, 69, 77, 80, 81, 85, 86, 169
Spanish vocabulary measure, 29, 34, 36, 42, 52, 63
Spanish-only education, 52, 89
St. Clair, R. N., 13, 171
Steinberg, Laurence D., 7, 9, 10, 20, 57, 171
Suárez-Orozco, Marcelo M., 12, 172

Teachner, Richard V., 22, 23, 172
Test of Adult Basic Education, 37, 172

Thompson, Roger M., 16, 17, 32, 172
Topic of conversation, 46, 69
Track, 4, 8, 27, 32, 54, 59, 76, 77, 83, 84, 169, 171
Trueba, Henry T., xi, 12, 25, 52, 165, 172, 173

U.S. House of Representatives, 5, 11, 19, 20, 21, 172
U.S. Department of Education, xi, xii, 6, 10, 14, 19, 25, 170, 172
Usdansky, M. L., 5, 6, 16, 20, 172

Valdés, Guadalupe, xiii, 172
Valdivieso, Rafael, xi, 4, 5, 6, 7, 8, 9, 16, 19, 54, 57, 83, 89, 172
Valenzuela de la Garza, J., 3, 11, 173
Valverde, Silvia A., 5, 6, 46, 89, 173
Vázquez, Marcherie, 173
Vélez, W., 7, 19, 173
Veltman, Calvin J., 10, 11, 14, 20, 22, 173

Walker, C. L., xi, 173
Watt, N. F., 12, 173
Weinreich, Uriel, 32, 173
Weller, G., 17, 23, 173
Wentz, J., 22, 173
Wright, John W., xv, 19, 48, 173, 174

Zentella, Ana Celia, xiii, 174